Hymns

The hymnal of the Inter-Varsity Christian Fellowship

Compiled and edited by Paul Beckwith

INTER-VARSITY CHRISTIAN FELLOWSHIP CHICAGO 1

First printing, 1947

Second printing, 1948

Christian singing for the thoughtful

S INGING is having a new impact on today's Christian life. Christians on campus and other members of their generation have rediscovered in music a satisfying expression of the thoughts of their souls and of the fellowship with Jesus Christ. Singing for them has become more than casual amusement—it has again become effective evangelism, humble prayer, clear testimony, and heartfelt worship.

This new understanding of Christian singing stems from ancient traditions—traditions that found in music a satisfying expression for sincere Christian thoughts, traditions that carefully united these honest words of the soul with fitting music, traditions which found a proper occasion for each of the several types of Christian songs.

Such understanding makes each song service an intrinsic part of any meeting and requires as careful a selection of hymns as of Scripture portions or of the speaker. It demands that the music be considered seriously in advance and that unpreparedness not be hidden behind the glib excuse, "Let's have your favorite selection."

Singing thus planned draws attention to the meaning of the song—and not to mere virility or volume. The song leader seeks to inspire reverence before God, to help the people begin their singing together, to keep them in the proper time—but he avoids the distractions of the cheer-leader technique. The pianist, likewise, makes more complete the joy of singing—without breaking the mood with attention-drawing flourishes.

Everyone given a proper opportunity loves a familiar song, but sometimes new songs like unfamiliar portions of Scripture need understanding introductions. An appropriate new song at every meeting brings new spiritual experiences. Attention should be drawn to the words of each new song, then to the music. If there is a story that will help in understanding the song, it should be told. Then everyone should join in singing all the stanzas—without mutilation of the thought in a hasty race to the finish.

'Hymns is planned to make such satisfying, natural singing more simple. Appropriate words and music have been brought together. The arrangement of the book is functional, with songs most appropriate for particular types of meetings grouped together. To make this feature of organization more usable, each section begins with a helpful introduction.

The editor wishes to express special appreciation to Mr. David Adeney of London for his valuable assistance in helping to procure English copyright permissions and to Mr. C. Stacey Woods. Thanks are given also to individuals and organizations which have permitted the use of their copyrighted words and music.

Every effort has been made to locate copyright owners and to secure proper permissions. In case of any errors or omissions, correction will be made gladly in subsequent edition of *Hymns*.

When you gather for Christian fellowship

WHEN CHRISTIANS gather together they usually want to sing. Sometimes they will want to praise the Lord; at other times they will want to express their confidence in Him; or they will want to sing together hymns of assurance, of victory, of faith in action.

This meeting should not be too formal. Let the spirit of the meeting dictate the hymns you sing. Have you had a special blessing from God? Then sing a hymn of praise. Has God given you a real victory in your personal life? Then sing a hymn that tells of your confidence in Him. Has God given your group a big task to perform? Then sing a song which speaks of vital faith—faith in action.

When life is difficult, let one of these hymns be a solo before God of your joyous confidence in Him.

O for a thousand tongues

CHARLES WESLEY   CARL G GLASER (LOWELL MASON, ARR.)

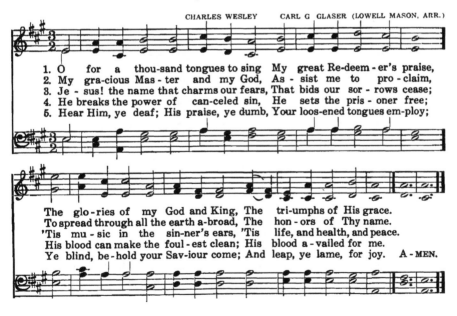

1. O for a thou-sand tongues to sing My great Re-deem-er's praise,
2. My gra-cious Mas-ter and my God, As-sist me to pro-claim,
3. Je-sus! the name that charms our fears, That bids our sor-rows cease;
4. He breaks the power of can-celed sin, He sets the pris-oner free;
5. Hear Him, ye deaf; His praise, ye dumb, Your loos-ened tongues em-ploy;

The glo-ries of my God and King, The tri-umphs of His grace.
To spread through all the earth a-broad, The hon-ors of Thy name.
'Tis mu-sic in the sin-ner's ears, 'Tis life, and health, and peace.
His blood can make the foul-est clean; His blood a-vailed for me.
Ye blind, be-hold your Sav-iour come; And leap, ye lame, for joy. A-MEN.

Will your anchor hold in the storms of life

PRISCILLA J. OWENS   WILLIAM J. KIRKPATRICK

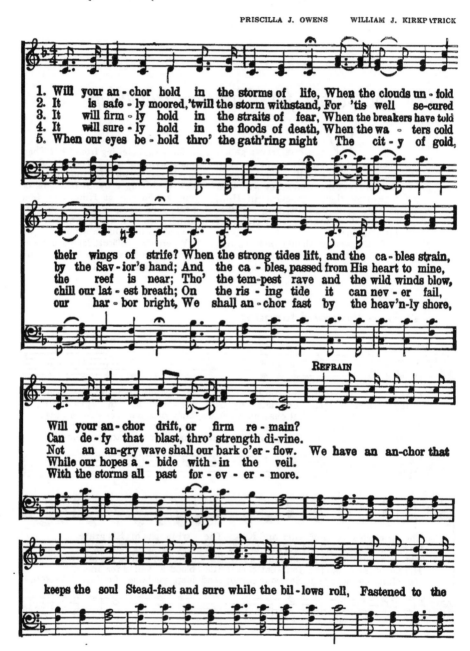

1. Will your an-chor hold in the storms of life, When the clouds un-fold
2. It is safe-ly moored,'twill the storm withstand, For 'tis well se-cured
3. It will firm-ly hold in the straits of fear, When the breakers have told
4. It will sure-ly hold in the floods of death, When the wa-ters cold
5. When our eyes be-hold thro' the gath'ring night The cit-y of gold,

their wings of strife? When the strong tides lift, and the ca-bles strain,
by the Sav-ior's hand; And the ca-bles, passed from His heart to mine,
the reef is near; Tho' the tem-pest rave and the wild winds blow,
chill our lat-est breath; On the ris-ing tide it can nev-er fail,
our har-bor bright, We shall an-chor fast by the heav'n-ly shore,

REFRAIN

Will your an-chor drift, or firm re-main?
Can de-fy that blast, thro' strength di-vine.
Not an an-gry wave shall our bark o'er-flow.   We have an an-chor that
While our hopes a-bide with-in the veil.
With the storms all past for-ev-er-more.

keeps the soul Stead-fast and sure while the bil-lows roll, Fastened to the

Rock which can-not move, Grounded firm and deep in the Sav-ior's love.

Thou wilt keep him in perfect peace 3

FROM SCRIPTURE   ANON. (PAUL BECKWITH, ARR.)

Thou wilt keep him in per - fect peace,

1. Thou wilt keep him in per - fect peace,   Thou wilt
2. Mar - vel not that I say un - to you,   Mar - vel
3. Tho' your sins as scar - let be,   Tho' your
4. If the Son shall make you free,   If the
5. They that wait up - on the Lord,   They that

Thou wilt keep him in per - fect peace,   Thou wilt

keep him in per - fect peace,   Thou wilt keep him in
not that I say un - to you,   Mar - vel not that I
sins as scar - let be,   Tho' your sins as
Son shall make you free,   If the Son shall
wait up - on the Lord,   They that wait up -

keep him in per - fect peace, Whose mind is stayed on Thee.

per - fect peace, Whose mind is stayed on Thee.____
say un - to you, Ye must be born a - gain.____
scar - let be, They shall be white as snow.____
make you free, Ye shall be free in - deed.____
on the Lord, They shall re - new their strength.____

Great is Thy faithfulness

THOMAS O. CHISHOLM   WILLIAM M. RUNYAN

1. "Great is Thy faith-ful-ness," O God my Fa-ther, There is no shad-ow of
2. Sum-mer and win-ter, and springtime and harvest, Sun, moon and stars in their
3. Par-don for sin and a peace that en-dur-eth, Thy own dear pres-ence to

turn-ing with Thee; Thou chang-est not, Thy com-pas-sion, they fail not;
cours-es a-bove, Join with all na-ture in man-i-fold wit-ness
cheer and to guide; Strength for to-day and bright hope for to-mor-row,

CHORUS

As Thou hast been Thou for-ev-er wilt be.
To Thy great faith-ful-ness, mer-cy and love. "Great is Thy faith-ful-ness!
Bless-ings all mine, with ten thou-sand be-side!

Great is Thy faithfulness!" Morning by morning new mer-cies I see; All I have

need-ed Thy hand hath pro-vid-ed—"Great is Thy faithfulness," Lord, un-to me!

rall.

PSALM 23 (GEORGE HERBERT, TR.)   FRIEDRICH SPEE

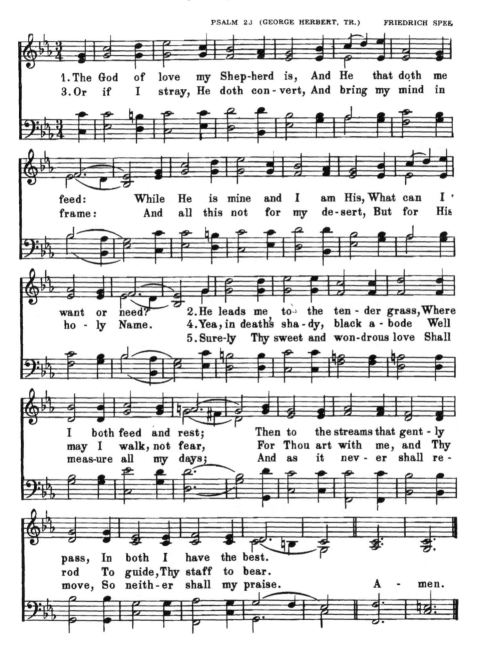

1. The God of love my Shep-herd is, And He that doth me
3. Or if I stray, He doth con-vert, And bring my mind in

feed: While He is mine and I am His, What can I
frame: And all this not for my de-sert, But for His

want or need?   2. He leads me to the ten-der grass, Where
ho-ly Name.   4. Yea, in death's sha-dy, black a-bode Well
   5. Sure-ly Thy sweet and won-drous love Shall

I both feed and rest; Then to the streams that gent-ly
may I walk, not fear, For Thou art with me, and Thy
meas-ure all my days; And as it nev-er shall re-

pass, In both I have the best.
rod To guide, Thy staff to bear.
move, So neith-er shall my praise.   A - men.

6   *I take Thy promise, Lord*

H. L. R. DECK   FROM F. C. GOUDIMEL

1. I take Thy prom - ise, Lord, in all its length,
   And breadth and ful - ness, as my dai - ly strength,
   In - to life's fu - ture fear - less I may gaze,
   For, Je - sus, Thou art with me all the days.

2. There may be days of dark - ness and dis - tress,
   When sin has pow'r to tempt, and care to press
   Yet in the dark - est day I will not fear,
   For, 'mid the shad - ows, Thou wilt still be near.

3. Days there may be of joy, and deep de - light,
   When earth seems fair - est, and her skies most bright;
   Then draw me clos - er to Thee, lest I rest
   Else - where, my Sav - iour, than up - on Thy breast.

4. And all the oth - er days that make my life,
   Mark'd by no spe - cial joy or grief or strife,
   Days fill'd with qui - et du - ties, triv - ial care,
   Bur - dens too small for oth - er hearts to share.

5. Spend Thou these days with me, all shall be Thine
   So shall the dark - est hour with glo - ry shine.
   Then when these earth - ly years have pass'd a - way,
   Let me be with Thee in the per - fect day. A - men.

Words by permission of Miss E. Deck

Unto the hills around do I lift up

PSALM 121   CHARLES H. PURDAY

1. Un - to the hills a - round do I lift up My long - ing eyes;
2. He will not suf - fer that thy foot be moved: Safe shalt thou be.
3. Je - ho - vah is Him - self thy keep - er true, Thy change-less shade;
4. From ev - ery e - vil shall He keep thy soul, From ev - ery sin;

O whence for me shall my sal - va - tion come, From whence a - rise?
No care - less slum - ber shall His eye - lids close, Who keep - eth thee.
Je - ho - vah thy de - fense on thy right hand Him - self hath made.
Je - ho - vah shall pre - serve thy go - ing out, Thy com - ing in.

From God the Lord doth come my cer - tain aid,
Be - hold, He sleep - eth not, He slum - bereth ne'er,
And thee no sun by day shall ev - er smite;
A - bove thee watch - ing, He whom we a - dore

From God the Lord who heaven and earth hath made.
Who keep - eth Is - rael in His ho - ly care.
No moon shall harm thee in the si - lent night.
Shall keep thee hence - forth, yea, for - ev - er - more. A-MEN.

8
Be still, my soul

KATHARINA VON SCHLEGEL (JANE L BORTHWICK, TR.)   JEAN SIBELIUS

1. Be still, my soul: the Lord is on thy side;   Bear pa-tient-ly the
2. Be still, my soul: thy God doth un-der-take   To guide the fu-ture
3. Be still, my soul: the hour is has-tening on   When we shall be for

cross of grief or pain; Leave to thy God to or-der and pro-vide;
as He has the past. Thy hope, thy con-fi-dence let noth-ing shake;
ev-er with the Lord, When dis-ap-point-ment, grief, and fear are gone,

In ev-ery change He faith-ful will re-main. Be still, my soul: thy
All now mys-te-rious shall be bright at last. Be still, my soul: the
Sor-row for-got, love's pur-est joys re-stored. Be still, my soul: when

best, thy heavenly Friend Thro thorn-y ways leads to a joy-ful end.
waves and winds still know His voice who ruled them while He dwelt be-low.
change and tears are past, All safe and bless-ed we shall meet at last. A-MEN.

Music by permission of Presbyterian Board of Christian Education, arr. from The Hymnal, 1933

We rest on Thee, our Shield and our Defender

EDITH G. CHERRY   TUNE OF HYMN 8

1. "We rest on Thee"—our Shield and our Defender!
   We go not forth alone against the foe;
   Strong in Thy strength, safe in Thy keeping tender,
   "We rest on Thee, and in Thy Name we go."

2. Yea, "in Thy Name," O Captain of salvation!
   In Thy dear Name, all other names above;
   Jesus our Righteousness, our sure Foundation,
   Our Prince of glory and our King of love.

3. "We go" in faith, our own great weakness feeling,
   And needing more each day Thy grace to know:
   Yet from our hearts a song of triumph pealing;
   "We rest on Thee, and in Thy name we go."

4. "We rest on Thee"—our Shield and our Defender!
   Thine is the battle, Thine shall be the praise
   When passing through the gates of pearly splendour,
   Victors—we rest *with* Thee, through endless days.

By permission of Marshall, Morgan and Scott, Ltd.

Fight the good fight

JOHN S B. MONSELL   WILLIAM BOYD

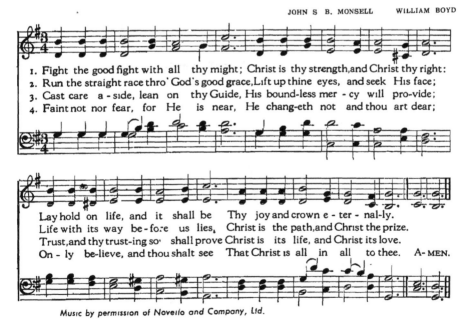

1. Fight the good fight with all thy might; Christ is thy strength, and Christ thy right:
2. Run the straight race thro' God's good grace, Lift up thine eyes, and seek His face;
3. Cast care a-side, lean on thy Guide, His bound-less mer-cy will pro-vide;
4. Faint not nor fear, for He is near, He chang-eth not and thou art dear;

Lay hold on life, and it shall be Thy joy and crown e-ter-nal-ly.
Life with its way be-fore us lies, Christ is the path, and Christ the prize.
Trust, and thy trust-ing so' shall prove Christ is its life, and Christ its love.
On-ly be-lieve, and thou shalt see That Christ is all in all to thee. A-MEN.

Music by permission of Novello and Company, Ltd.

The Lord's my Shepherd, I'll not want

PSALM 23   TRADITIONAL ENGLISH MELODY

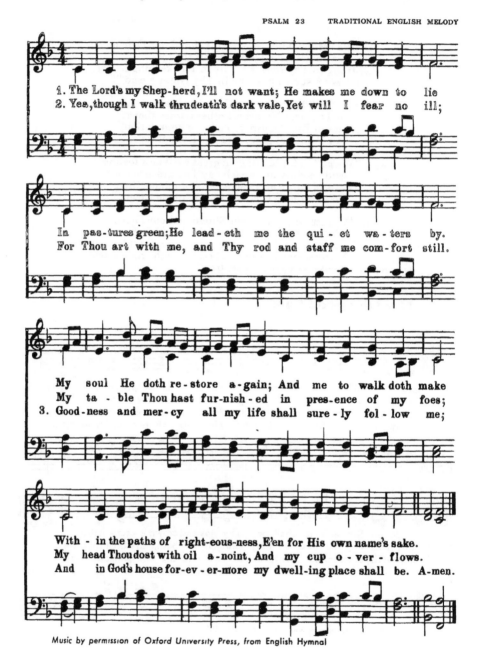

1. The Lord's my Shep-herd, I'll not want; He makes me down to lie
2. Yea, though I walk thru death's dark vale, Yet will I fear no ill;

In pas-tures green; He lead-eth me the qui-et wa-ters by.
For Thou art with me, and Thy rod and staff me com-fort still.

My soul He doth re-store a-gain; And me to walk doth make
My ta-ble Thou hast fur-nish-ed in pres-ence of my foes;
3. Good-ness and mer-cy all my life shall sure-ly fol-low me;

With-in the paths of right-eous-ness, E'en for His own name's sake.
My head Thou dost with oil a-noint, And my cup o-ver-flows.
And in God's house for-ev-er-more my dwell-ing place shall be. A-men.

Music by permission of Oxford University Press, from English Hymnal

ROBERT M MC CHEYNE   RICHARD REDHEAD

1. When this pass - ing world is done, When has sunk yon
2. When I stand be - fore the throne Dress'd in beau - ty
3. E'en on earth, as through a glass, Dark - ly, let Thy
4. Cho - sen not for good in me, Wak - en'd up from

glo - rious sun, When we stand with Christ on high,
not my own, When I see Thee as Thou art,
glo - ry pass; Make for - give - ness feel so sweet;
wrath to flee; Hid - den in the Sav - iour's side,

Look - ing o'er life's his - to - ry; Then, Lord, shall I
Love Thee with un - sin - ning heart; Then, Lord, shall I
Make Thy Spir - it's help so meet; E'en on earth, Lord,
By the Spir - it sanc - ti - fied; Teach me, Lord, on

ful - ly know Not till then how much I owe.
ful - ly know Not till then how much I owe.
make me know Some-thing of how much I owe.
earth to show, By my love, how much I owe. A-men.

If thou but suffer God to guide thee

GEORG NEUMARK (CATHERINE WINKWORTH, TR)   GEORG NEUMARK

1. If thou but suf - fer God to guide thee, And hope in
2. O - bey, thou rest - less heart, be still   And wait in
3. Sing, pray, and swerve not from His ways;   But do thine

Him thro' all thy ways, He'll give the strength, what-e'er be - tide
cheer - ful hope, con - tent To take what-e'er His gra - cious will,
own part faith-ful - ly. Trust His rich prom - is - es of grace,

thee, And bear thee thro the e - vil days; Who trusts in God's un -
His all dis - cern-ing love, hath sent; Nor doubt our in - most
So shall they be ful-filled in thee. God nev - er yet for -

chang-ing love Builds on the rock that naught can move.
wants are known To Him who chose us for His own.
sook in need The soul that trust-ed Him in-deed. A - men.

By grace I am an heir of heaven

CHR. LUDWIG SCHEIT (H. BREUCKNER, TR.)   TUNE OF HYMN 13

1. By grace I am an heir of heaven:
   Why doubt this, O my trembling
      heart?
   If what the Scriptures promise
      clearly
   Is true and firm in ev'ry part,
   This also must be truth divine:
   By grace a crown of life is thine.

2. By grace alone shall I inherit
   That blissful home beyond the
      skies.
   Works count for naught, the Lord
      incarnate
   Hath won for me the heav'nly
      prize.
   Salvation by His death He
      wrought,
   His grace alone my pardon bought.

3. By grace! These precious words re-
      member
   When sorely by thy sins oppressed,
   When Satan comes to vex thy
      spirit,
   When troubled conscience sighs
      for rest;
   What reason cannot comprehend,
   God doth to thee by grace extend.

4. By grace! Be this in death my com-
      fort;
   Despite my fears, 'tis well with me.
   I know my sin in all its greatness,
   But also Him who sets me free.
   My heart to naught but joy gives
      place
   Since I am saved by grace, by
      grace.

Jesus, and shall it ever be

JOSEPH GRIGG   FRANCIS DUCKWORTH

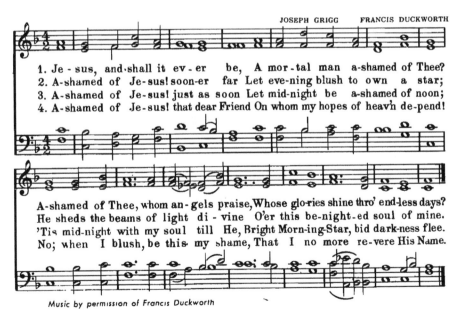

1. Je-sus, and shall it ev-er be, A mor-tal man a-shamed of Thee?
2. A-shamed of Je-sus! soon-er far Let eve-ning blush to own a star;
3. A-shamed of Je-sus! just as soon Let mid-night be a-shamed of noon;
4. A-shamed of Je-sus! that dear Friend On whom my hopes of heav'n de-pend!

A-shamed of Thee, whom an-gels praise, Whose glo-ries shine thro' end-less days?
He sheds the beams of light di - vine O'er this be-night-ed soul of mine.
'Tis mid-night with my soul till He, Bright Morn-ing-Star, bid dark-ness flee.
No; when I blush, be this my shame, That I no more re-vere His Name.

The sands of time are sinking

ANNE R. COUSIN   CHRETIAN D'URHAN (E. F. RIMBAULT, ARR.)

1. The sands of time are sink - ing, The dawn of heav - en breaks,
2. Oh, Christ, He is the foun - tain, The deep, sweet well of love!
3. With mer - cy and with judg - ment My web of time He wove,
4. The bride eyes not her gar - ment, But her dear bride-groom's face;

The sum - mer morn I've sighed for, The fair, sweet morn a - wakes.
The streams of earth I've tast - ed; More deep I'll drink a - bove.
And aye the dews of sor - row Were lus - tered with His love:
I will not gaze at glo - ry, But on my King of grace;

O dark hath been the mid - night, But day - spring is at hand,
There to an o - cean full - ness His mer - cy doth ex - pand,
I'll bless the hand that guid - ed, I'll bless the heart that planned
Not at the crown He giv - eth, But on His pierc - ed hand:

And glo - ry, glo - ry dwell - eth In Em - man - uel's land.
And glo - ry, glo - ry dwell - eth In Em - man - uel's land.
When throned where glo - ry dwell - eth in Em - man - uel's land.
The Lamb is all the glo - ry Of Em - man - uel's land.

W. H. BURLEIGH   FRIEDRICH F. FLEMMING

1. Still will we trust, though earth seem dark and
2. Our eyes see dim - ly 'til by faith a -
3. Choose for us, God, nor let our weak pre -
4. Let us press on, in pa - tient self de -

drear - y, And the heart faint be - neath His cha - st'ning
noint - ed, And our blind choos - ing brings us grief and
fer - ring Cheat us of good Thou hast for us de -
ni - al, Ac - cept the hard - ship, shrink not from the

rod; Though rough and steep our path - way, worn and
pain; Through Him a - lone, who hath our way ap -
signed: Choose for us, God; Thy wis - dom is un -
loss: Our por - tion lies be - yond the hour of

wea - ry, Still will we trust in God.
point - ed, We find our peace a - gain.
err - ing. And we are fools and blind.
tri - al, Our crown be - yond the cross. A - men.

Beneath the cross of Jesus

ELIZABETH C. CLEPHANE   FREDERICK C. MAKER

1. Be - neath the cross of Je - sus I fain would take my stand,
2. Up - on that cross of Je - sus Mine eye at times can see
3. I take, O cross, thy shad - ow For my a - bid - ing place;

The shad - ow of a might - y rock With - in a wea - ry land;
The ver - y dy - ing form of One Who suf - fered there for me;
I ask no oth - er sun - shine than The sun - shine of His face;

A home with - in the wil - der - ness, A rest up - on the way,
And from my strick - en heart with tears Two won - ders I con - fess:
Con - tent to let the world go by, To know no gain nor loss,

From the burn - ing of the noon - tide heat, And the bur - den of the day.
The won - ders of re - deem - ing love And my un - wor - thi - ness.
My sin - ful self my on - ly shame, My glo - ry all the cross. A - MEN.

JOACHIM MAGDEBURG   ARTHUR S. SULLIVAN

1. Who trusts in God, a strong a-bode In heaven and earth pos-sess-es;
2. Though sa-tan's wrath be-set our path, And world-ly scorn as-sail us,
3. In all the strife of mor-tal life Our feet shall stand se-cure-ly;

Who looks in love to Christ a-bove, No fear his heart op-press-es.
While Thou art near we will not fear, Thy strength shall nev-er fail us:
Temp-ta-tion's hour shall lose its power, For Thou shalt guard us sure-ly.

In Thee a-lone, dear Lord, we own Sweet hope and con-so-la-tion;
Thy rod and staff shall keep us safe, And guide our steps for ev-er;
O God, renew, with heavenly dew, Our bod-y, soul, and spir-it,

Our shield from foes, our balm for woes, Our great and sure sal-va-tion.
Nor shades of death, nor hell be-neath, Our souls from Thee shall sev-er.
Un-til we stand at Thy right hand, Through Jesus' sav-ing mer-it.

Music by permission of Novello and Company, Ltd.

Shall I empty-handed be

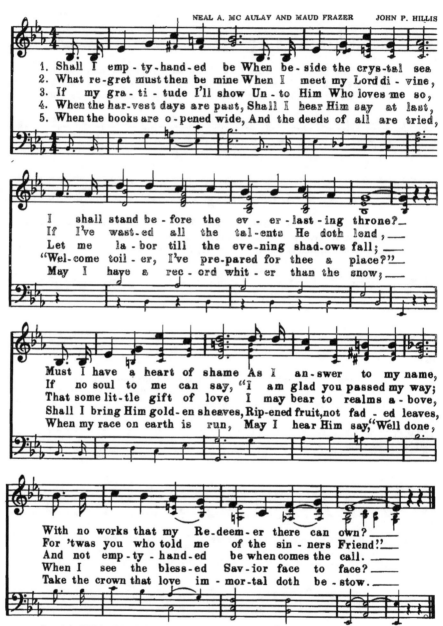

NEAL A. MC AULAY AND MAUD FRAZER   JOHN P. HILLIS

1. Shall I emp - ty-hand-ed be When be - side the crys-tal sea
2. What re-gret must then be mine When I meet my Lord di - vine,
3. If my gra - ti - tude I'll show Un - to Him Who loves me so,
4. When the har-vest days are past, Shall I hear Him say at last,
5. When the books are o-pened wide, And the deeds of all are tried,

I shall stand be - fore the ev - er - last - ing throne?
If I've wast-ed all the tal-ents He doth lend,
Let me la - bor till the eve-ning shad-ows fall;
"Wel-come toil - er, I've pre-pared for thee a place?"
May I have a rec - ord whit - er than the snow;

Must I have a heart of shame As I an - swer to my name,
If no soul to me can say, "I am glad you passed my way;
That some lit-tle gift of love I may bear to realms a - bove,
Shall I bring Him gold-en sheaves, Rip-ened fruit, not fad - ed leaves,
When my race on earth is run, May I hear Him say, "Well done,

With no works that my Re-deem-er there can own?
For 'twas you who told me of the sin - ners Friend?"
And not emp-ty - hand-ed be when comes the call.
When I see the bless-ed Sav-ior face to face?
Take the crown that love im - mor-tal doth be - stow.

JOHN E. BODE   JAMES W. ELLIOTT

1. O Je - sus, I have prom - ised To serve Thee to the end;
2. Oh! let me feel Thee near me; The world is ev - er near;
3. O Je - sus, Thou hast prom - ised To all who fol - low Thee,

Be Thou for - ev - er near me, My Mas - ter and my Friend!
I see the sights that daz - zle, The tempt - ing sounds I hear.
That where Thou art in glo - ry There shall Thy ser - vant be;

I shall not fear the bat - tle, If Thou art by my side,
My foes are ev - er near me, A - round me and with - in;
And, Je - sus, I have prom - ised To serve Thee to the end;

Voices in Unison   In Harmony

Nor wan - der from the path - way, If Thou wilt be my Guide.
But, Je - sus, draw Thou near - er, And shield my soul from sin.
Oh! give me grace to fol - low My Mas - ter and my Friend!

4. Oh! let me hear Thee speaking
   In accents clear and still,
  Above the storms of passion,
   The murmurs of self-will:

Oh! speak to re-assure me,
  To hasten or control;
Oh! speak, and make me listen,
  Thou Guardian of my soul.

A mighty fortress is our God

MARTIN LUTHER (FREDERICK H. HEDGE, TR.)   MARTIN LUTHER

1. A might-y Fortress is our God, A Bul-wark nev-er fail - ing;
2. Did we in our own strength con-fide, Our striv-ing would be los - ing;
3. And though this world, with dev-ils filled, Should threat-en to un - do us;
4. That word a - bove all earth-ly powers, No thanks to them, a - bid - eth;

Our Help-er He a - mid the flood Of mor-tal ills pre - vail - ing:
Were not the right Man on our side, The Man of God's own choos - ing:
We will not fear, for God hath willed His truth to tri - umph through us:
The Spir - it and the gifts are ours Through Him who with us sid - eth:

For still our an-cient Foe Doth seek to work us woe; His craft and power are great,
Dost ask who that may be? Christ Je-sus, it is He; Lord Sab-a-oth His Name,
The Prince of Dark-ness grim, We trem-ble not for him; His rage we can en - dure,
Let goods and kin-dred go, This mor-tal life al - so; The bod-y they may kill:

And, armed with cru - el hate, On earth is not his e - qual.
From age to age the same, And He must win the bat - tle
For lo! his doom is sure, One lit - tle word shall fell him.
God's truth a - bid - eth still, His King-dom is for - ev - er. A-MEN.

PSALM 136 (ISAAC WATTS. TR.) GEISTLICHE KIRCHENGESANG

1. Give to our God im-mor-tal praise! Mer-cy and truth are all His
2. Give to the Lord of lords re-nown, The King of kings with glo-ry
3. He saw the Gen-tiles dead in sin, And felt his pit-y work with-
4. He sent His Son with pow'r to save, From guilt, and dark-ness, and the

ways; Al-le-lu-ia! Al-le-lu-ia! Won-ders of grace to God be-
crown; Al-le-lu-ia! Al-le-lu-ia! His mer-cies ev-er shall en-
in; Al-le-lu-ia! Al-le-lu-ia! His mer-cies ev-er shall en-
grave; Al-le-lu-ia! Al-le-lu-ia! Won-ders of grace to God be-

long, Re-peat His mer-cies in your song. Al-le-lu-ia! Al-le-
dure, When lords and kings are known no more. Al-le-lu-ia! Al-le-
dure, When death and sin shall reign no more. Al-le-lu-ia! Al-le-
long, Re-peat His mer-cies in your song. Al-le-lu-ia! Al-le-

lu-ia! Al-le-lu-ia! Al-le-lu-ia! Al-le-lu-ia! A-men.

MATTHEW BRIDGES   GEORGE J. ELVEY

1. Crown Him with man - y crowns, The Lamb up - on His throne;
2. Crown Him the Lord of life, Who tri - umphed o'er the grave,
3. Crown Him the Lord of peace, Whose power a scep - ter sways
4. Crown Him the Lord of love; Be - hold His hands and side,

Hark! how the heaven-ly an - them drowns All mu - sic but its own.
And rose vic - to - rious in the strife For those He came to save;
From pole to pole, that wars may cease, And all be prayer and praise:
Those wounds, yet vis - i - ble a - bove, In beau - ty glo - ri - fied:

A - wake, my soul, and sing Of Him who died for thee,
His glo - ries now we sing Who died, and rose on high,
His reign shall know no end, And round His pierc - ed feet
All hail, Re - deem - er, hail! For Thou hast died for me:

And hail Him as thy match-less King Through all e - ter - ni - ty.
Who died — e - ter - nal life to bring, And lives, that death may die.
Fair flowers of par - a - dise ex - tend Their fra-grance ev - er sweet.
Thy praise and glo - ry shall not fail Through-out e - ter - ni - ty. A-MEN.

Soldiers of Christ, arise

CHARLES WESLEY   TUNE OF HYMN 24

1. Soldiers of Christ, arise,
   And put your armour on,
   Strong in the strength which God supplies
   Through His eternal Son:
   Strong in the Lord of hosts,
   And in His mighty power:
   Who in the strength of Jesus trusts
   Is more than conqueror.

2. Stand then in His great might,
   With all His strength endued;
   And take, to arm you for the fight,
   The panoply of God.
   That, having all things done,
   And all your conflicts past,
   Ye may o'ercome through Christ alone,
   And stand complete at last.

3. From strength to strength go on,
   Wrestle, and fight, and pray;
   Tread all the powers of darkness down,
   And win the well-fought day:
   Still let the Spirit cry,
   In all His soldiers, "Come,"
   Till Christ the Lord descend from high,
   And take the conquerors home.

Lord, in the fulness of my might

THOMAS H. GILL   C. E. MILLER

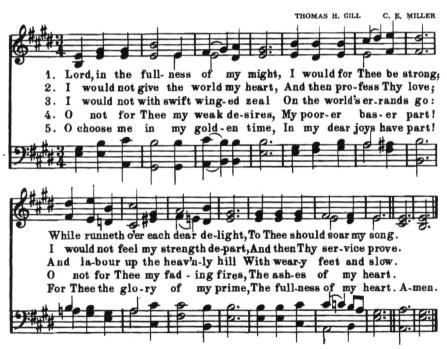

1. Lord, in the full-ness of my might, I would for Thee be strong;
2. I would not give the world my heart, And then pro-fess Thy love;
3. I would not with swift wing-ed zeal On the world's er-rands go:
4. O not for Thee my weak de-sires, My poor-er bas-er part!
5. O choose me in my gold-en time, In my dear joys have part!

While runneth o'er each dear de-light, To Thee should soar my song.
I would not feel my strength de-part, And then Thy ser-vice prove.
And la-bour up the heav'n-ly hill With wear-y feet and slow.
O not for Thee my fad-ing fires, The ash-es of my heart.
For Thee the glo-ry of my prime, The full-ness of my heart. A-men.

FRANCES R. HAVERGAL   ANON. (JOHN GOSS ARR.)

1. Who is on the Lord's side? Who will serve the King? Who will be His
2. Not for weight of glo - ry, Not for crown and palm, En - ter we the
3. Je - sus, Thou hast bought us, Not with gold or gem, But with Thine own
4. Fierce may be the con - flict, Strong may be the foe, But the King's own

help - ers Oth - er lives to bring? Who will leave the world's side?
ar - my, Raise the war - rior psalm; But for love that claim - eth
life - blood, For Thy di - a - dem. With Thy bless - ing fill - ing
ar - my, None can o - ver - throw. Round His stand-ard rang - ing

Who will face the foe? Who is on the Lord's side? Who for
Lives for whom He died; He whom Je - sus nam - eth Must be
Each who comes to Thee, Thou hast made us will - ing, Thou hast
Vic - tory is se - cure; For His truth un - chang-ing Makes the

Him will go? By Thy call of mer - cy, By Thy grace di - vine,
on His side. By Thy love con - strain-ing, By Thy grace di - vine,
made us free. By Thy grand re - demp-tion, By Thy grace di - vine,
tri - umph sure. Joy - ful - ly en - list - ing By Thy grace di - vine,

We are on the Lord's side, Sav - iour, we are Thine. A - men.

REGINALD HEBER   HENRY S. CUTLER

1. The Son of God goes forth to war, A king-ly crown to gain;
2. The mar-tyr first, whose ea-gle eye Could pierce be-yond the grave,
3. A glo-rious band, the cho-sen few On whom the Spir-it came,
4. A no-ble ar-my, men and boys, The ma-tron and the maid,

His blood-red ban-ner streams a-far: Who fol-lows in His train?
Who saw his Mas-ter in the sky, And called on Him to save:
Twelve va-liant saints, their hope they knew, And mocked the cross and flame:
A-round the Sav-iour's throne re-joice, In robes of light ar-rayed:

Who best can drink his cup of woe, Tri-um-phant o-ver pain,
Like Him, with par-don on his tongue In midst of mor-tal pain,
They met the ty-rant's brandished steel, The li-on's go-ry mane;
They climbed the steep as-cent of heaven Through per-il, toil, and pain;

Who pa-tient bears his cross be-low, He fol-lows in His train.
He prayed for them that did the wrong: Who fol-lows in his train?
They bowed their necks the death to feel: Who fol-lows in their train?
O God, to us may grace be given To fol-low in their train. A-MEN.

The Church's one foundation

SAMUEL J STONE   SAMUEL S. WESLEY

1. The Church-'s one foun - da - tion   Is   Je - sus Christ her Lord;
2. E - lect from ev - ery na - tion,   Yet one o'er all   the earth,
3. 'Mid toil and trib - u - la - tion,   And tu - mult of her war,
4. Yet she   on earth hath un - ion   With God the Three in One,

She   is   His new cre - a - tion   By   wa - ter and the word;
Her char - ter of   sal - va - tion,   One Lord, one faith, one birth;
She waits the con - sum - ma - tion   Of   peace for ev - er - more;
And mys - tic sweet com - mun - ion   With those whose rest   is   won:

From heaven He came and sought her   To   be   His ho - ly   bride;
One   ho - ly Name she bless - es,   Par - takes one ho - ly   food,
Till,   with the vi - sion glo - rious,   Her long - ing eyes are blest,
O   hap - py ones and   ho - ly!   Lord, give   us grace that we,

With His own blood He bought her, And for   her life He died.
And   to   one hope she press - es, With ev - ery grace en - dued.
And   the great Church vic - to - rious Shall be   the Church at rest.
Like them, the meek and low - ly, On high may dwell with Thee.   A - MEN.

OSWALD J SMITH   DANIEL B. TOWNER

1. For sal - va - tion full and free, Pur-chased once on Cal - va - ry,
2. He my Guide from day to day, As I jour-ney on life's way;
3. May my Mod - el ev - er be Christ the Lord, and none save He,
4. He shall reign from shore to shore; His the glo - ry ev - er-more—

Christ a - lone shall be my plea— Je - sus! Je - sus on - ly.
Close be - side Him let me stay— Je - sus! Je - sus on - ly.
That the world may see in me— Je - sus! Je - sus on - ly.
Heav'n and earth shall bow be - fore— Je - sus! Je - sus on - ly.

CHORUS

Je - sus on - ly, let me see, Je - sus on - ly, none save He,

Then my song shall ev - er be— Je - sus! Je - sus on - ly!

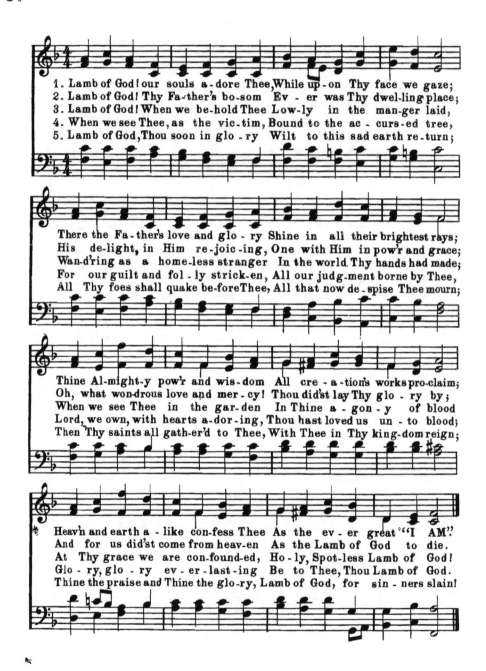

1. Lamb of God! our souls a-dore Thee, While up-on Thy face we gaze;
2. Lamb of God! Thy Fa-ther's bo-som Ev - er was Thy dwel-ling place;
3. Lamb of God! When we be-hold Thee Low-ly in the man-ger laid;
4. When we see Thee, as the vic-tim, Bound to the ac - curs-ed tree,
5. Lamb of God, Thou soon in glo - ry Wilt to this sad earth re-turn;

There the Fa-ther's love and glo - ry Shine in all their brightest rays;
His de-light, in Him re-joic-ing, One with Him in pow'r and grace;
Wan-d'ring as a home-less stranger In the world Thy hands had made;
For our guilt and fol - ly strick-en, All our judg-ment borne by Thee,
All Thy foes shall quake be-fore Thee, All that now de-spise Thee mourn;

Thine Al-might-y pow'r and wis-dom All cre - a-tion's works pro-claim;
Oh, what won-drous love and mer-cy! Thou did'st lay Thy glo-ry by;
When we see Thee in the gar-den In Thine a-gon-y of blood
Lord, we own, with hearts a-dor-ing, Thou hast loved us un-to blood;
Then Thy saints all gath-er'd to Thee, With Thee in Thy king-dom reign;

Heav'n and earth a - like con-fess Thee As the ev - er great "I AM".
And for us did'st come from heav-en As the Lamb of God to die.
At Thy grace we are con-found-ed, Ho-ly, Spot-less Lamb of God!
Glo - ry, glo - ry ev - er-last-ing Be to Thee, Thou Lamb of God.
Thine the praise and Thine the glo-ry, Lamb of God, for sin - ners slain!

Jesus, wond'rous Saviour!

D. A. MC GREGOR

THOMAS HASTINGS

1. Je - sus, won - d'rous Sav - iour! Christ, of kings the King!
2. All earth's flow-ing pleas - ures Were a win - try sea,
3. Life is death, if sev - ered From Thy throb-bing heart.
4. Je - sus! all per - fec - tions Rise and end in Thee;

An - gels fall be - fore Thee, Pros-trate, wor - ship-ping;
Heav'n it - self with-out Thee Dark as night would be.
Death with life a - bund-ant At Thy touch would start.
Bright-ness of God's glo - ry Thou, e - ter - nal - ly.

Fair - est they con-fess Thee In the Heav'n a - bove.
Lamb of God! Thy glo - ry Is the light a - bove.
Worlds and men and an - gels All con - sist in Thee:
Fav - our'd be-yond meas - ure They Thy face who see;

We would sing Thee fair - est Here in hymns of love;
Lamb of God! Thy glo - ry Is the life of love.
Yet Thou cam - est to us In hu - mil - i - ty.
May we, gra - cious Sav - iour, Share this ec - sta - sy.

The "McMaster Hymn"; by permission

PSALM 91 (JAMES MONTGOMERY. TR.) ROWLAND H. PRICHARD

Call Je - ho - vah thy sal - va - tion, Rest be - neath th'Al - might - y's shade,
From the sword at noon-day wast-ing, From the noi-some pes - ti - lence,
Since with pure and firm af - fec - tion, Thou on God hast set thy love,

In His se - cret hab - i - ta - tion Dwell and nev - er be dis-mayed:
In the depth of mid-night blast-ing, God shall be thy sure de - fense:
With the wings of His pro - tec - tion He will shield thee from a - bove:

There no tu - mult shall a - larm thee, Thou shalt dread no hid - den snare;
He shall charge His an-gel le - gions Watch and ward o'er thee to keep;
Thou shalt call on Him in trou - ble, He will heark-en, He will save;

Guile nor vi - o - lence can harm thee, In e - ter-nal safe-guard there.
Tho' thou walk thro' lonesome regions, Tho' in des-ert wilds thou sleep.
Here for grief re-ward thee dou - ble, Crown with life be-yond the grave. Amen.

ISAAC WATTS   JOHN DARWALL

1. Join all the glo-rious names Of wis-dom, love, and power,
2. Great Pro-phet of my God, My tongue would bless Thy Name:
3. Je - sus, my great High Priest, Of - fered His blood, and died;
4. I love my Shep-herd's voice: His watch-ful eye shall keep
5. My Sav - ior and my Lord, My Con-quer'r and my King,

That ev - er mor - tals knew, That an - gels
By Thee the joy - ful news Of our sal -
My guilt - y con - science seeks No sac - ri -
My wan - d'ring soul a - mong The thou - sands
Thy scep - tre and Thy sword, Thy reign - ing

ev - er bore: All are too mean to speak His worth,
va - tion came, The joy - ful news of sins for-giv'n
fice be - side: His pow'r-ful blood did once a - tone
of His sheep: He feeds His flock, He calls their names,
grace I sing: Thine is the pow'r; be-hold I sit

Too mean to set my Sav - iour forth.
Of hell sub - dued and peace with heav'n.
And now it pleads be - fore the throne.
His bos - om bears the ten - der lambs.
In will - ing bonds be - neath Thy feet. A - men.

JOHN H. YATES   IRA D. SANKEY

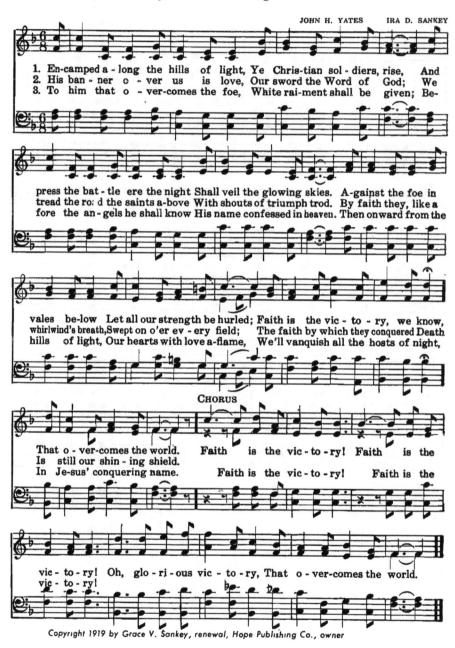

1. En-camped a - long the hills of light, Ye Chris-tian sol - diers, rise, And
2. His ban - ner o - ver us is love, Our sword the Word of God; We
3. To him that o - ver-comes the foe, White rai-ment shall be given; Be-

press the bat - tle ere the night Shall veil the glowing skies. A-gainst the foe in
tread the ro; d the saints a-bove With shouts of triumph trod. By faith they, like a
fore the an - gels he shall know His name confessed in heaven. Then onward from the

vales be-low Let all our strength be hurled; Faith is the vic - to - ry, we know,
whirlwind's breath, Swept on o'er ev - ery field; The faith by which they conquered Death
hills of light, Our hearts with love a-flame, We'll vanquish all the hosts of night,

CHORUS

That o - ver-comes the world.   Faith is the vic - to - ry! Faith is the
Is still our shin - ing shield.
In Je-sus' conquering name.   Faith is the vic - to - ry!   Faith is the

vic - to - ry! Oh, glo - ri - ous vic - to - ry, That o - ver-comes the world.
vic - to - ry!

FANNY J. CROSBY　　CHESTER G ALLEN

1. Praise Him! praise Him! Je-sus, our bless-ed Re-deem-er! Sing, O Earth, His
2. Praise Him! praise Him! Je-sus, our bless-ed Re-deem-er! For our sins He
3. Praise Him! praise Him! Je-sus, our bless-ed Re-deem-er! Heavenly por-tals

won-der-ful love pro-claim! Hail Him! hail Him! highest archangels in glo-ry;
suffered, and bled and died; He our Rock, our hope of e-ter-nal sal-va-tion,
loud with ho-san-nas ring! Je-sus, Sav-iour, reigneth for-ev-er and ev-er;

Strength and hon-or give to His ho-ly name! Like a shep-herd Je-sus will
Hail Him! hail Him! Je-sus the Cru-ci-fied. Sound His prais-es! Je-sus who
Crown Him! crown Him! Prophet and Priest and King! Christ is com-ing! o-ver the

REFRAIN

guard His children, In His arms He carries them all day long:
bore our sor-rows; Love unbounded, wonderful, deep and strong: Praise Him! praise Him!
world vic-to-rious, Power and glo-ry un-to the Lord be-long:

tell of His ex-cel-lent greatness; Praise Him! praise Him! ever in joy-ful song!

Praise, my soul, the King of heaven

HENRY F LYTE · JOHN GOSS

1. Praise, my soul, the King of heav - en, To His feet thy
2. Praise Him for His grace and fa - vor To our fa - thers
3. Fa - ther - like, He tends and spares us, Well our fee - ble
4. An - gels, help us to a - dore Him, Ye be - hold Him

trib - ute bring; Ran - somed, healed, re - stored, for - giv - en,
in dis - tress; Praise Him, still the same for ev - er,
frame He knows; In His hands He gen - tly bears us,
face to face; Sun and moon, bow down be - fore Him,

Who, like me, His praise should sing? Al - le - lu - ia!
Slow to chide, and swift to bless; Al - le - lu - ia!
Res - cues us from all our foes, Al - le - lu - ia!
Dwell - ers all in time and space, Al - le - lu - ia!

Al - le - lu - ia! Praise the ev - er - last - ing King!
Al - le - lu - ia! Glo - rious in His faith - ful - ness!
Al - le - lu - ia! Wide - ly as His mer - cy flows!
Al - le - lu - ia! Praise with us the God of grace! A-MEN.

Look, ye saints, the sight is glorious

THOMAS KELLY   TUNE OF HYMN 37

1. Look, ye saints, the sight is glorious
   See the "Man of Sorrows" now
   From the fight return victorious:
   Every knee to Him shall bow!
   Crown Him! crown Him!
   Crowns become the Victor's brow.

2. Crown the Saviour! angels, crown Him!
   Rich·the trophies Jesus brings;
   In the seat of power enthrone Him,
   While the vault of heaven rings!
   Crown Him! crown Him!
   Crown the Saviour "King of kings."

3. Sinners in derision crowned Him,
   Mocking thus the Saviour's claim;
   Saints and angels crowd around Him,
   Own His title, praise His Name.
   Crown Him! crown Him!
   Spread abroad the Victor's fame.

4. Hark, the bursts of acclamation!
   Hark, those loud triumphant chords!
   Jesus takes the highest station,
   Oh, what joy the sight affords!
   Crown Him! crown Him,
   "King of kings, and Lord of lords!"

Praise the Saviour, ye who know Him!

THOMAS KELLY   TRADITIONAL GERMAN MELODY

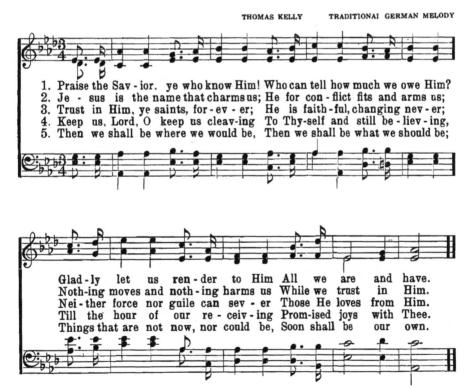

1. Praise the Sav - ior. ye who know Him! Who can tell how much we owe Him?
2. Je - sus is the name that charms us; He for con - flict fits and arms us;
3. Trust in Him, ye saints, for - ev - er; He is faith - ful, changing nev - er;
4. Keep us, Lord, O keep us cleav - ing To Thy-self and still be - liev - ing,
5. Then we shall be where we would be, Then we shall be what we should be;

Glad - ly let us ren - der to Him All we are and have.
Noth - ing moves and noth - ing harms us While we trust in Him.
Nei - ther force nor guile can sev - er Those He loves from Him.
Till the hour of our re - ceiv - ing Prom - ised joys with Thee.
Things that are not now, nor could be, Soon shall be our own.

40 Like a river glorious

FRANCES. R. HAVERGAL   J. MOUNTAIN

1. Like a riv - er, glo - rious Is God's per - fect peace, O - ver all vic -
2. Hid - den in the hol - low Of His bless - ed hand, Nev - er foe can
3. Ev - ery joy or tri - al Fall - eth from a - bove, Traced up - on our

to - rious In its bright in - crease; Per - fect, yet it flow - eth
fol - low, Nev - er trai - tor stand; Not a surge of wor - ry,
di - al By the Sun of Love. We may trust Him ful - ly

CHORUS — Stayed up - on Je - ho - vah,
Chorus, D.S.

Full -er ev - ery day, Per - fect, yet it grow - eth Deep - er all the way.
Not a shade of care, Not a blast of hur - ry Touch the spir - it there.
All for us to do; They who trust Him whol - ly Find Him whol - ly true. A - MEN.

Hearts are ful - ly blest; Find - ing, as He prom - ised, Per - fect peace and rest.

41 Jesus shall reign where'er the sun

ISAAC WATTS   JOHN HATTON

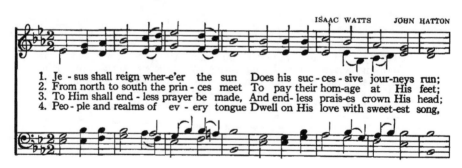

1. Je - sus shall reign wher - e'er the sun Does his suc - ces - sive jour - neys run;
2. From north to south the prin - ces meet To pay their hom - age at His feet;
3. To Him shall end - less prayer be made, And end - less prais - es crown His head;
4. Peo - ple and realms of ev - ery tongue Dwell on His love with sweet - est song,

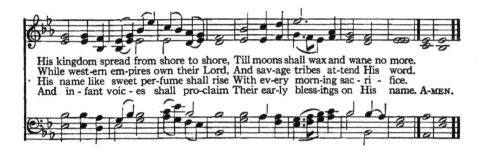

His kingdom spread from shore to shore, Till moons shall wax and wane no more.
While west-ern em-pires own their Lord, And sav-age tribes at-tend His word.
His name like sweet per-fume shall rise With ev-ery morn-ing sac - ri - fice.
And in - fant voic - es shall pro-claim Their ear-ly bless-ings on His name. A-MEN.

Holy, holy, holy, Lord God Almighty 42

REGINALD HEBER   JOHN B. DYKES

1. Ho - ly, ho - ly, ho - ly, Lord God Al-might - y! Ear - ly in the
2. Ho - ly, ho - ly, ho - ly! all the saints a - dore Thee, Cast-ing down their
3. Ho - ly, ho - ly, ho - ly! tho' the dark-ness hide Thee, Tho' the eye of
4. Ho - ly, ho - ly, ho - ly, Lord God Al-might - y! All Thy works shall

morn - ing our song shall rise to Thee; Ho - ly, ho - ly, ho - ly,
gold-en crowns a - round the crys - tal sea; Cher-u - bim and sera - phim
sin- ful men Thy glo - ry may not see; On - ly Thou art ho - ly;
praise Thy name, in earth, and sky, and sea; Ho - ly, ho - ly, ho - ly,

mer - ci - ful and might-y! God in Three Per- sons, blessed Trin-i-ty!
fall-ing down be - fore Thee, Who wast, and art, and ev-er-more shalt be.
there is none be-side Thee, Per-fect in pow'r, in love, and pu-ri - ty.
mer - ci - ful and might-y! God in Three Per- sons, blessed Trin-i-ty! A-MEN.

All hail the power of Jesus' name

EDWARD PERRONET   JAMES ELLOR

1. All hail the power of Je - sus' name! Let an - gels pros-trate
2. Ye cho - sen seed of Is - rael's race; Ye ran-somed from the
3. Sin - ners, whose love can ne'er for - get The worm-wood and the
4. Let ev - ery kin - dred, ev - ery tribe, On this ter - res - trial
5. O that with yon - der sa - cred throng We at His feet may

fall, Let an - gels pros - trate fall; Bring forth the roy - al
fall, Ye ran - somed from the fall; Hail Him who saves you
gall, The worm - wood and the gall, Go, spread your tro - phies
ball, On this ter - res - trial ball, To Him all maj - es -
fall, We at His feet may fall! We'll join the ev - er -

di - a - dem, And crown . . . . Him,
by His grace, And crown . . . . Him,
at His feet, And crown . . . . Him,
ty as - cribe, And crown . . . . Him,
last - ing song, And crown . . . . Him,

crown Him,   crown Him,   crown Him,   crown Him,

crown . . .

crown Him, crown Him, crown Him, And crown Him Lord of all. A - MEN.

. . . . Him.

When you speak of Christ to others

THERE IS no place where it is more important to have the right song service than at a meeting where you are introducing your friends to Christ. You choose your speaker with infinite care—you should choose your Gospel hymns the same way; you like personal witnessing that rings true—make sure that your songs of testimony are also sincere.

When you want to tell others about Christ, there are three general types of hymns that you can use: Gospel hymns which tell God's plan and provision of salvation through faith in Christ and His finished work; testi-mony hymns which declare to others what Christ means to you and what He has done for you; and invitation hymns which present Christ's call to trust in Him.

Gospel hymns are appropriate whenever Christ's salvation message is emphasized. Songs of testimony are often helpful. They are suitable when you present Christ to others, and also in your devotional meetings. Do not neglect the wide variety of invitation hymns in this section. Perhaps more people have trusted Christ during the singing of a hymn than at any other time.

Amazing grace! how sweet the sound   44

JOHN NEWTON   TRADITIONAL AMERICAN MELODY

1. A - maz - ing grace! how sweet the sound, That saved a wretch like me!
2. 'Twas grace that taught my heart to fear, And grace my fears re - lieved;
3. Thro' man - y dan - gers, toils, and snares, I have al - read - y come;
4. The Lord has prom-ised good to me, His word my hope se - cures;
5. When we've been there ten thou-sand years, Bright shin-ing as the sun,

I once was lost, but now am found, Was blind, but now I see.
How pre - cious did that grace ap - pear The hour I first be - lieved!
'Tis grace hath bro't me safe thus far, And grace will lead me home.
He will my shield and por - tion be As long as life en - dures.
We've no less days to sing God's praise, Than when we first be - gun. A-men.

I've found a Friend; O such a Friend!

JAMES G. SMALL   ARTHUR SULLIVAN

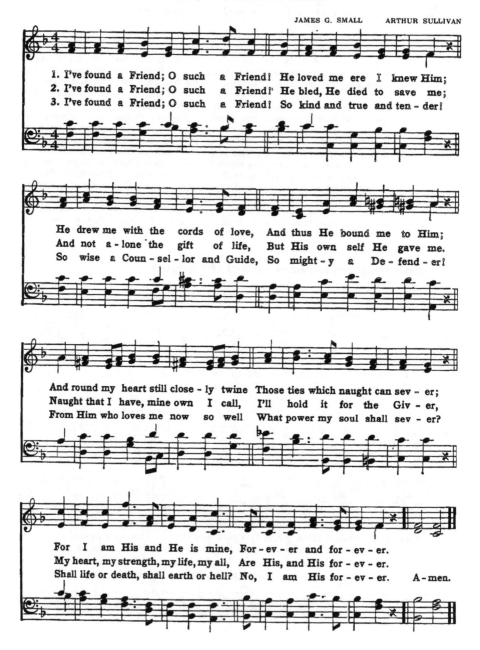

1. I've found a Friend; O such a Friend! He loved me ere I knew Him;
2. I've found a Friend; O such a Friend! He bled, He died to save me;
3. I've found a Friend; O such a Friend! So kind and true and ten-der!

He drew me with the cords of love, And thus He bound me to Him;
And not a-lone the gift of life, But His own self He gave me.
So wise a Coun-sel-lor and Guide, So might-y a De-fend-er!

And round my heart still close-ly twine Those ties which naught can sev-er;
Naught that I have, mine own I call, I'll hold it for the Giv-er,
From Him who loves me now so well What power my soul shall sev-er?

For I am His and He is mine, For-ev-er and for-ev-er.
My heart, my strength, my life, my all, Are His, and His for-ev-er.
Shall life or death, shall earth or hell? No, I am His for-ev-er. A-men.

W. T SLEEPER   GEORGE C. STEBBINS

1. Out of my bond-age, sor-row and night, Je-sus, I come, Je-sus, I come;
2. Out of my shame-ful fail-ure and loss, Je-sus, I come, Je-sus, I come;
3. Out of un-rest and ar-ro-gant pride, Je-sus, I come, Je-sus, I come;
4. Out of the fear and dread of the tomb, Je-sus, I come, Je-sus, I come;

In-to Thy free-dom, glad-ness and light, Je-sus, I come to Thee;
In-to the glo-rious gain of Thy cross, Je-sus, I come to Thee;
In-to Thy bless-ed will to a-bide, Je-sus, I come to Thee;
In-to the joy and light of Thy home, Je-sus, I come to Thee;

Out of my sick-ness in-to Thy health, Out of my want and in-to Thy wealth,
Out of earth's sorrows into Thy balm, Out of life's storms and in-to Thy calm,
Out of my-self to dwell in Thy love, Out of de-spair in-to rap-tures a-bove,
Out of the depths of ru-in un-told, In-to the peace of Thy sheltering fold,

Out of my sin and in-to Thy-self, Je-sus, I come to Thee.
Out of dis-tress to ju-bi-lant psalm, Je-sus, I come to Thee.
Up-ward for aye on wings like a dove, Je-sus, I come to Thee.
Ev-er Thy glo-rious face to be-hold, Je-sus, I come to Thee.   A-MEN.

When we walk with the Lord

J. H. SAMMIS   DANIEL B. TOWNER

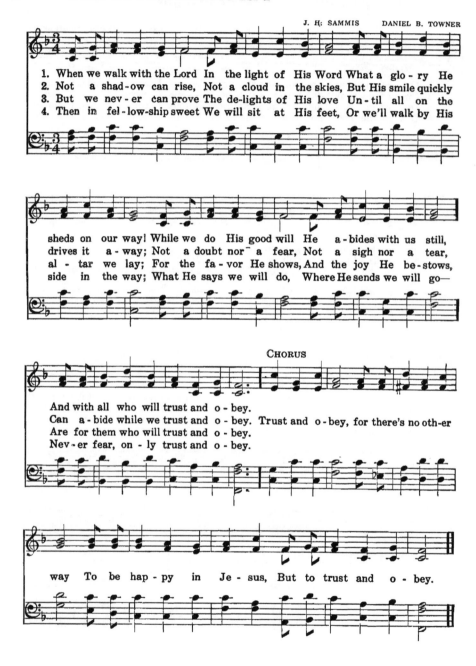

1. When we walk with the Lord In the light of His Word What a glo-ry He
2. Not a shad-ow can rise, Not a cloud in the skies, But His smile quickly
3. But we nev-er can prove The de-lights of His love Un-til all on the
4. Then in fel-low-ship sweet We will sit at His feet, Or we'll walk by His

sheds on our way! While we do His good will He a-bides with us still,
drives it a-way; Not a doubt nor a fear, Not a sigh nor a tear,
al-tar we lay; For the fa-vor He shows, And the joy He be-stows,
side in the way; What He says we will do, Where He sends we will go—

CHORUS

And with all who will trust and o-bey.
Can a-bide while we trust and o-bey. Trust and o-bey, for there's no oth-er
Are for them who will trust and o-bey.
Nev-er fear, on-ly trust and o-bey.

way To be hap-py in Je-sus, But to trust and o-bey.

EDWARD MOTE WILLIAM B. BRADBURY

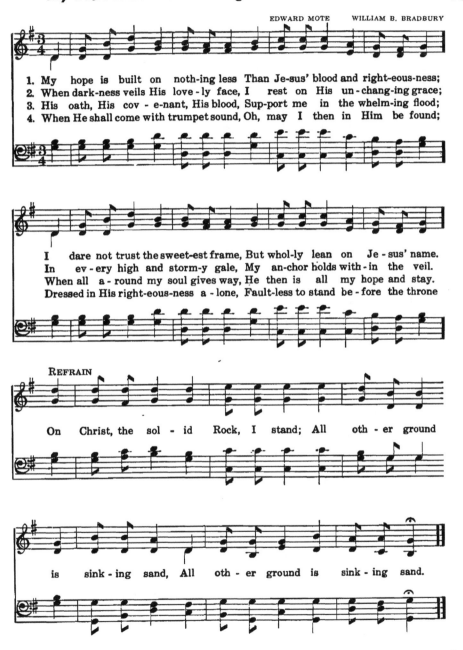

1. My hope is built on noth-ing less Than Je-sus' blood and right-eous-ness;
2. When dark-ness veils His love-ly face, I rest on His un-chang-ing grace;
3. His oath, His cov-e-nant, His blood, Sup-port me in the whelm-ing flood;
4. When He shall come with trumpet sound, Oh, may I then in Him be found;

I dare not trust the sweet-est frame, But whol-ly lean on Je-sus' name.
In ev-ery high and storm-y gale, My an-chor holds with-in the veil.
When all a-round my soul gives way, He then is all my hope and stay.
Dressed in His right-eous-ness a-lone, Fault-less to stand be-fore the throne

REFRAIN

On Christ, the sol-id Rock, I stand; All oth-er ground

is sink-ing sand, All oth-er ground is sink-ing sand.

9

In tenderness He sought me

W. SPENCER WALTON   ADONIRAM J. GORDON

1. In ten - der - ness He sought me, Wea - ry and sick with sin,
2. He wash'd the bleed - ing sin - wounds, And poured in oil and wine;
3. He point - ed to the nail - prints, For me His blood was shed,
4. I'm sit - ting in His pres - ence, The sun - shine of His face,
5. So while the hours are pass - ing, All now is per - fect rest,

And on His shoul - ders brought me, Back to His fold a - gain.
He whis - pered to as - sure me, "I've found thee, thou art Mine;"
A mock - ing crown so thorn - y, Was placed up - on His head:
While with a - dor - ing won - der His bless - ings I re - trace.
I'm wait - ing for the morn - ing, The bright - est and the best,

While an - gels in His pres-ence sang Un - til the courts of Heav - en rang.
I nev - er heard a sweet - er voice, It made my ach - ing heart re - joice!
I won-dered what He saw in me, To suf - fer such deep ag - o - ny.
It seems as if e - ter - nal days Are far too short to sound His praise.
When He will call us to His side, To be with Him, His spot - less bride.

CHORUS

Oh, the love that sought me! Oh, the blood that bought me, Oh, the grace that

brought me to the fold, Won-drous grace that brought me to the fold!

I sought the Lord, and afterward I knew

50

ANON. GEORGE W. CHADWICK

1 I sought the Lord, and af-ter-ward I knew He moved my
2 Thou didst reach forth Thy hand and mine en-fold; I walked and
3 I find, I walk, I love; but O the whole Of love is

soul to seek Him, seek-ing me; It was not I that
sank not on the storm-vexed sea; 'Twas not so much that
but my an-swer, Lord, to Thee! For Thou wert long be-

found, O Sav-ior true; No, I was found of Thee.
I on Thee took hold, As Thou, dear Lord, on me.
fore-hand with my soul; Al-ways Thou lov-edst me.

To God be the glory

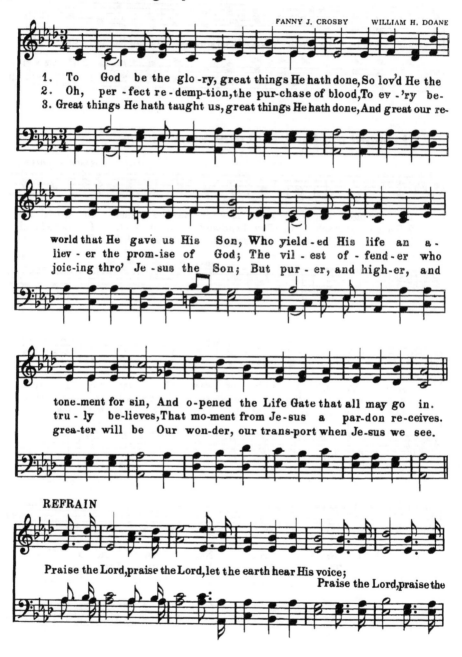

FANNY J. CROSBY   WILLIAM H. DOANE

1. To God be the glo-ry, great things He hath done, So lov'd He the
2. Oh, per-fect re-demp-tion, the pur-chase of blood, To ev-'ry be-
3. Great things He hath taught us, great things He hath done, And great our re-

world that He gave us His Son, Who yield-ed His life an a-
liev-er the prom-ise of God; The vil-est of-fend-er who
joic-ing thro' Je-sus the Son; But pur-er, and high-er, and

tone-ment for sin, And o-pened the Life Gate that all may go in.
tru-ly be-lieves, That mo-ment from Je-sus a par-don re-ceives.
grea-ter will be Our won-der, our trans-port when Je-sus we see.

REFRAIN

Praise the Lord, praise the Lord, let the earth hear His voice;
Praise the Lord, praise the

Lord, let the peo-ple re-joice; Oh, come to the Fa-ther, thro'

Je-sus the Son, And give Him the glo-ry; great things He hath done.

Prove Him! an almighty Saviour

52

ANON.   EBENEZER PROUT

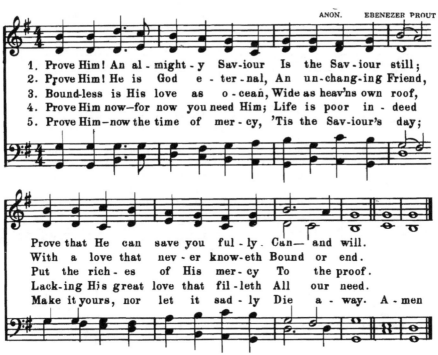

1. Prove Him! An al-might-y Sav-iour Is the Sav-iour still;
2. Prove Him! He is God e-ter-nal, An un-chang-ing Friend,
3. Bound-less is His love as o-cean, Wide as heav'ns own roof,
4. Prove Him now—for now you need Him; Life is poor in-deed
5. Prove Him—now the time of mer-cy, 'Tis the Sav-iour's day;

Prove that He can save you ful-ly. Can— and will.
With a love that nev-er know-eth Bound or end.
Put the rich-es of His mer-cy To the proof.
Lack-ing His great love that fil-leth All our need.
Make it yours, nor let it sad-ly Die a-way. A-men

By permission of the Congregational Union of England and Wales

CHARLOTTE ELLIOTT   HENRY SMART

1. Just as I am, with-out one plea, But that Thy
2. Just as I am, and wait-ing not To rid my
3. Just as I am, tho' tossed a - bout With man-y a
4. Just as I am, poor, wretch-ed, blind, Sight, rich-es,
5. Just as I am, Thou wilt re-ceive, Wilt wel-come,

blood was shed for me, And that Thou bid'st me
soul of one dark blot, To Thee, whose blood can
con - flict, man - y a doubt, Fight-ings with - in, and
heal - ing of the mind, Yea, all I need, in
par - don, cleanse, re - lieve; Be-cause Thy prom - ise

come to Thee, O Lamb of God I come!
cleanse each spot, O Lamb of God I come!
fears with - out, O Lamb of God I come!
Thee to find, O Lamb of God I come!
I be - lieve, O Lamb of God I come!

6 Just as I am, Thy love unknown
Hath broken ev'ry barrier down;
Now to be Thine, yea Thine alone,
O Lamb of God I come.

7 Just as I am, of that free love
The breadth, length, depth, the
  height to prove,
Here for a season, then above,
O Lamb of God I come.

JOSEPH H. GILMORE   WILLIAM B. BRADBURY

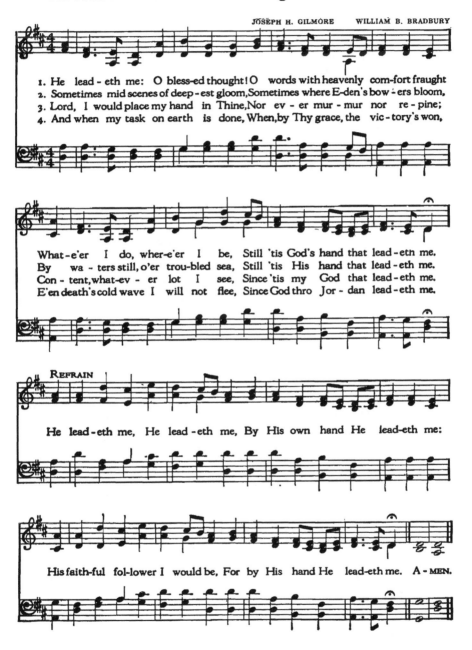

1. He lead-eth me: O bless-ed thought! O words with heavenly com-fort fraught
2. Sometimes mid scenes of deep-est gloom, Sometimes where E-den's bow-ers bloom,
3. Lord, I would place my hand in Thine, Nor ev-er mur-mur nor re-pine;
4. And when my task on earth is done, When, by Thy grace, the vic-tory's won,

What-e'er I do, wher-e'er I be, Still 'tis God's hand that lead-eth me.
By wa-ters still, o'er trou-bled sea, Still 'tis His hand that lead-eth me.
Con-tent, what-ev-er lot I see, Since 'tis my God that lead-eth me.
E'en death's cold wave I will not flee, Since God thro Jor-dan lead-eth me.

REFRAIN

He lead-eth me, He lead-eth me, By His own hand He lead-eth me:

His faith-ful fol-lower I would be, For by His hand He lead-eth me. A-MEN.

S TREVOR FRANCIS   T. J. WILLIAMS

1. O the deep, deep love of Je - sus, Vast, un - meas - ured,
bound - less, free; Roll - ing as a might - y o - cean In its
full - ness o - ver me. Un - der - neath me, all a - round me,
Is the cur - rent of Thy love; Lead - ing on - ward, lead - ing
home - ward, To my glo - rious rest a - bove.

2. O the deep, deep love of Je - sus, Spread His praise from
shore to shore; How He lov - eth, ev - er lov - eth, Chang - eth
nev - er, nev - er more; How He watch - es o'er His loved ones,
Died to call them all His own; How for them He in - ter -
ced - eth, Watch - eth o'er them from the throne.

3. O the deep, deep love of Je - sus, Love of ev - 'ry
love the best; 'Tis an o - cean vast of bless - ing, 'Tis a
ha - ven sweet of rest, O the deep, deep love of Je - sus,
'Tis a Heav'n of Heav'ns to me; And it lifts me up to
glo - ry, For it lifts me up to Thee. A - men.

Music by permission of W. Gwenlyn Evans and Sons

JOHN NEWTON   ALEXANDER R. REINAGLE

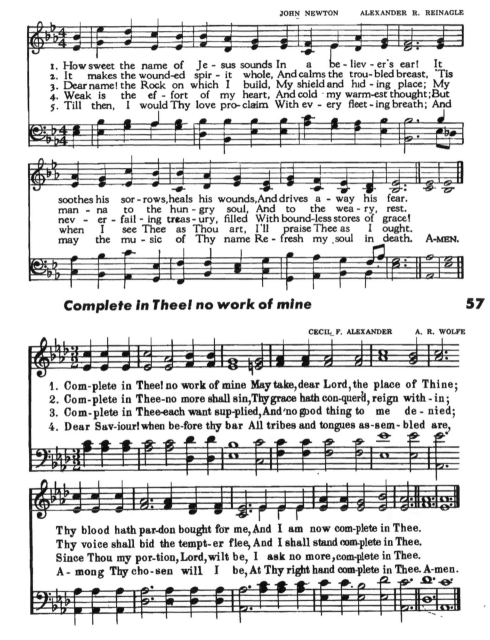

1. How sweet the name of Je - sus sounds In a be - liev - er's ear! It
2. It makes the wound-ed spir - it whole, And calms the trou-bled breast, 'Tis
3. Dear name! the Rock on which I build, My shield and hid - ing place; My
4. Weak is the ef - fort of my heart, And cold my warm-est thought; But
5. Till then, I would Thy love pro-claim With ev - ery fleet-ing breath; And

soothes his sor - rows, heals his wounds, And drives a - way his fear.
man - na to the hun - gry soul, And to the wea - ry, rest.
nev - er - fail - ing treas-ury, filled With bound-less stores of grace!
when I see Thee as Thou art, I'll praise Thee as I ought.
may the mu - sic of Thy name Re - fresh my soul in death. A-MEN.

Complete in Thee! no work of mine 57

CECIL F. ALEXANDER   A. R. WOLFE

1. Com-plete in Thee! no work of mine May take, dear Lord, the place of Thine;
2. Com-plete in Thee-no more shall sin, Thy grace hath con-quer'd, reign with - in;
3. Com-plete in Thee-each want sup-plied, And 'no good thing to me de - nied;
4. Dear Sav-iour! when be-fore thy bar All tribes and tongues as-sem - bled are,

Thy blood hath par-don bought for me, And I am now com-plete in Thee.
Thy voice shall bid the tempt- er flee, And I shall stand com-plete in Thee.
Since Thou my por-tion, Lord, wilt be, I ask no more, com-plete in Thee.
A - mong Thy cho-sen will I be, At Thy right hand com-plete in Thee. A-men.

M. PETERS   TRADITIONAL WELSH MELODY

1. Through the love of God our Sav-iour, All will be well;
2. Though we pass through tri - bu - la - tion, All will be well;
3. We ex-pect a bright to - mor-row, All will be well;

Free and change-less is His fa - vor, All, all is well;
Ours is such a full sal - va - tion, All, all is well;
Faith can sing, through days of sor-row, All, all is well;

Pre-cious is the blood that heal'd us, Per-fect is the grace that seal'd us,
Hap-py, still in God con-fid - ing, Fruit-ful, if in Christ a - bid - ing
On our Fa-ther's love re - ly - ing, Je - sus ev'-ry need sup-ply-ing,

Strong the hand stretch'd out to shield us, All must be well.
Ho - ly, through the Spir - it's guid-ing, All must be well.
Or in liv - ing or in dy - ing, All must be well.   A-men.

DANIEL W. WHITTLE   JAMES MC GRANAHAN

1. I know not why God's won-drous grace To me He hath made known,
2. I know not how this sav - ing faith To me He did im - part,
3. I know not how the Spir - it moves, Con-vinc-ing men of sin,
4. I know not what of good or ill May be re-served for me,
5. I know not when my Lord may come, At night or noon-day fair,

Nor why, un - wor - thy, Christ in love Re-deemed me for His own.
Nor how be - liev - ing in His Word Wrought peace within my heart.
Re - veal-ing Je - sus thro' the Word, Cre - at - ing faith in Him.
Of wea - ry ways or gold - en days, Be - fore His face I see.
Nor if I'll walk the vale with Him, Or "meet Him in the air."

CHORUS

But "I know whom I have be - liev - ed, and am per-suad-ed that He is

a - ble To keep that which I've com-mit-ted Un-to Him a-gainst that day."

ALFRED H. ACKLEY   ALFRED H. ACKLEY

1. I serve a ris - en Sav - ior, He's in the world to-day; I know that He is
2. In all the world a-round me I see His lov - ing care, And tho' my heart grows
3. Re-joice, re-joice, O Christian, lift up your voice and sing E - ter-nal hal - le -

liv - ing, what-ev - er men may say; I see His hand of mer - cy, I
wea - ry I nev - er will de - spair; I know that He is lead-ing, thro'
lu - jahs to Je - sus Christ the King! The Hope of all who seek Him, the

hear His voice of cheer, And just the time I need Him He's al-ways near.
all the storm-y blast, The day of His ap-pear-ing will come at last.
Help of all who find, None oth-er is so lov - ing, so good and kind.

REFRAIN *Spirited*

He lives,   He lives,   Christ Je-sus lives to - day! He walks with me and
He lives,   He lives,

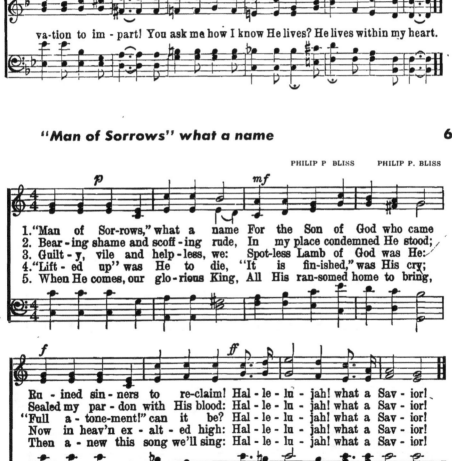

talks with me a-long life's nar-row way. He lives, He lives, sal-
He lives, He lives,

rit. ff

va-tion to im - part! You ask me how I know He lives? He lives within my heart.

"Man of Sorrows" what a name

PHILIP P BLISS   PHILIP P. BLISS

p   *mf*

1. "Man of Sor-rows," what a name For the Son of God who came
2. Bear-ing shame and scoff-ing rude, In my place condemned He stood;
3. Guilt-y, vile and help-less, we: Spot-less Lamb of God was He:
4. "Lift-ed up" was He to die, "It is fin-ished," was His cry;
5. When He comes, our glo-rious King, All His ran-somed home to bring,

f   *ff*

Ru - ined sin - ners to re-claim! Hal-le-lu - jah! what a Sav - ior!
Sealed my par - don with His blood: Hal-le-lu - jah! what a Sav - ior!
"Full a-tone-ment!" can it be? Hal-le-lu - jah! what a Sav - ior!
Now in heav'n ex - alt - ed high: Hal-le-lu - jah! what a Sav - ior!
Then a - new this song we'll sing: Hal-le-lu - jah! what a Sav - ior!

Once far from God and dead in sin

DANIEL W WHITTLE   JAMES MC GRANAHAN

1. Once far from God and dead in sin, No light my heart could see;
2. As rays of light from yon-der sun, The flow'rs of earth set free,
3. As lives the flow'r with-in the seed, As in the cone the tree,
4. With long-ing all my heart is filled, That like Him I may be,

But in God's Word the light I found, Now Christ liv-eth in me.
So life and light and love came forth From Christ liv-ing in me.
So, praise the God of truth and grace, His Spir-it dwell-eth in me.
As on the won-drous tho't I dwell That Christ liv-eth in me.

CHORUS

Christ liv-eth in me, Christ liv-eth in me,
Christ liv-eth in me, Christ liv-eth in

Oh! what a sal-va-tion this, That Christ liv-eth in me.
me, Oh!

Thou didst leave Thy throne

EMILY E S. ELLIOTT   TIMOTHY R. MATTHEWS

1. Thou didst leave Thy throne and Thy king - ly crown, When Thou
2. Heav - en's arch - es rang when the an - gels sang, Pro -
3. The fox - es found rest, and the birds their nest In the
4. Thou cam'st, O Lord, with the liv - ing word That should
5. When heaven's arch - es shall ring and her choir shall sing At Thy

cam - est to earth for me; But in Beth - le - hem's home there was
claim - ing Thy roy - al de - gree; But in low - ly birth didst Thou
shade of the for - est tree; But Thy couch was the sod, O Thou
set Thy peo - ple free; But with mock - ing scorn, and with
com - ing to vic - to - ry, Let Thy voice call me home, say - ing,

found no room For Thy ho - ly Na - tiv - i - ty. O
come to earth, And in great hu - mil - i - ty. O
Son of God, In the des - erts of Gal - i - lee. O
crown of thorn, They bore Thee to Cal - va - ry. O
"Yet there is room, There is room at my side for thee!" And my

come to my heart, Lord Je - sus, There is room in my heart for Thee.
come to my heart, Lord Je - sus, There is room in my heart for Thee.
come to my heart, Lord Je - sus, There is room in my heart for Thee.
come to my heart, Lord Je - sus, There is room in my heart for Thee.
heart shall re - joice, Lord Je - sus, When Thou com - est and callest for me. A-MEN.

God calling yet! Shall I not hear?

G. TERSTEEGEN (JANE BORTHWICK, TR.)   HENRY OLIVER

1. God call-ing yet! Shall I not hear? Earth's pleasures shall I still hold dear?
2. God call-ing yet! Shall I not rise? Can I His lov-ing voice de-spise,
3. God call-ing yet! And shall He knock, And I my heart the clos-er lock?
4. God call-ing yet! And shall I give No heed, but still in bond-age live?
5. God call-ing yet! I can-not stay; My heart I yield with-out de-lay:

Shall life's swift pass-ing years all fly, And still my soul in slum-ber lie?
And base-ly His kind care re-pay? He calls me still—can I de-lay?
He still is wait-ing to re-ceive, And shall I dare His Spir-it grieve?
I wait, but He does not for-sake; He calls me still—my heart, a-wake!
Vain world, farewell, from thee I part; The voice of God hath reached my heart. A-MEN.

Depth of mercy! can there be

CHARLES WESLEY   CARL M. VON WEBER

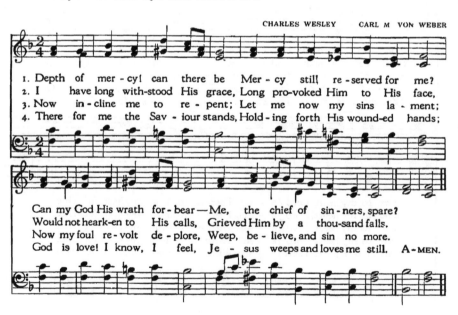

1. Depth of mer-cy! can there be Mer-cy still re-served for me?
2. I have long with-stood His grace, Long pro-voked Him to His face,
3. Now in-cline me to re-pent; Let me now my sins la-ment;
4. There for me the Sav-iour stands, Hold-ing forth His wound-ed hands;

Can my God His wrath for-bear—Me, the chief of sin-ners, spare?
Would not heark-en to His calls, Grieved Him by a thou-sand falls.
Now my foul re-volt de-plore, Weep, be-lieve, and sin no more.
God is love! I know, I feel, Je-sus weeps and loves me still. A-MEN.

O come, O come, Emmanuel

66

LATIN HYMN (JOHN M. NEALE, TR.) ANCIENT PLAIN SONG

1. O come, O come, Em - man - u - el, And ran - som cap - tive
2. O come, Thou Day-spring, come and cheer Our spir - its by Thine
3. O come, Thou Key of Da - vid, come, And o - pen wide our

Is - ra - el, That mourns in lone - ly ex - ile here
ad - vent here; Dis - perse the gloom - y clouds of night,
heaven - ly home; Make safe the way that leads on high,

Harmony

Un - til the Son of God ap - pear. Re - joice! Re - joice! Em -
And death's dark shad - ows put to flight. Re - joice! Re - joice! Em -
And close the path to mis - er - y. Re - joice! Re - joice! Em -

Unison

man - u - el Shall come to thee, O Is - ra - el!
man - u - el Shall come to thee, O Is - ra - el!
man - u - el Shall come to thee, O Is - ra - el! A-MEN.

67   In the cross of Christ I glory

JOHN BOWRING   JOHN STAINER

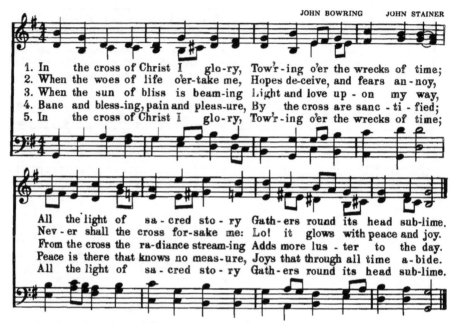

1. In   the cross of Christ I   glo-ry, Tow'r-ing o'er the wrecks of time;
2. When the woes of life o'er-take me, Hopes de-ceive, and fears an-noy,
3. When the sun of bliss is beam-ing Light and love up-on   my way,
4. Bane and bless-ing, pain and pleas-ure, By   the cross are sanc-ti-fied;
5. In   the cross of Christ I   glo-ry, Tow'r-ing o'er the wrecks of time;

All the light of   sa-cred sto-ry Gath-ers round its head sub-lime.
Nev-er shall the cross for-sake me: Lo! it   glows with peace and joy.
From the cross the ra-diance stream-ing Adds more lus-ter   to   the day.
Peace is there that knows no meas-ure, Joys that through all time a-bide.
All the light of   sa-cred sto-ry Gath-ers round its head sub-lime.

Music by permission of Novello and Company, Ltd.

68   Souls of men, why will ye scatter

FREDERICK W. FABER   TUNE OF HYMN 67

1. Souls of men, why will ye scatter
    Like a crowd of frightened sheep?
Foolish hearts, why will ye wander
    From a love so true and deep?

2. Was there ever kindest shepherd
    Half so gentle, half so sweet,
As the Saviour who would have us
    Come and gather round His feet?

3. There's a wideness in God's mercy
    Like the wideness of the sea,
There's a kindness in his justice
    Which is more than liberty.

4. There is welcome for the sinner,
    And more graces for the good;
There is mercy with the Saviour
    There is healing in His blood.

5. There is plentiful redemption
    In the blood that has been shed;
There is joy for all the members
    In the sorrows of the Head.

6. For the love of God is broader
    Than the measures of man's mind;
And the heart of the Eternal
    Is most wonderfully kind.

7. But we make His love too narrow
    By false limits of our own;
And we magnify its strictness
    With a zeal He will not own.

8. If our love were but more simple
    We should take Him at His word:
And our lives would be all sunshine
    In the sweetness of our Lord.

JULIA H. JOHNSTON   DANIEL B TOWNER

1. Mar - vel-ous grace of our lov - ing Lord, Grace that ex - ceeds our
2. Sin and de - spair like the sea waves cold, Threat-en the soul with
3. Dark is the stain that we can - not hide, What can a - vail to
4. Mar - vel - ous, in - fi - nite, match-less grace, Free - ly be-stowed on

sin and our guilt, Yon - der on Cal - va - ry's mount out-poured,
in - fi - nite loss; Grace that is great - er, yes, grace un - told,
wash it a - way? Look! there is flow - ing a crim - son tide;
all who 'be - lieve; You that are long - ing to see His face,

Chorus

There where the blood of the Lamb was spilt.
Points to the Ref - uge, the might - y Cross. Grace, grace,
Whit - er than snow you may be to - day.
Will you this mo - ment His grace re - ceive? Mar - vel - ous grace,

Cod's grace, Grace that will par-don and cleanse with-in; Grace,
in - fi-nite grace, Mar - vel-ous

grace, God's grace, Grace that is great - er than all our sin
grace, in - fi - nite grace,

Copyright 1938 by Ada P. Towner, renewal; Hope Publishing Co., owner

70 One day

J WILBUR CHAPMAN   CHARLES H. MARSH

1. One day when heav-en was filled with His prais-es, One day when
2. One day they led Him up Cal-va-ry's moun-tain, One day they
3. One day they left Him a-lone in the gar-den, One day He
4. One day the grave could con-ceal Him no lon-ger, One day the
5. One day the trump-et will sound for His com-ing, One day the

sin was as black as could be, Je-sus came forth to be
nailed Him to die on the tree; Suf-fer-ing an-guish, de-
rest-ed, from suf-fer-ing free; An-gels came down o'er His
stone rolled a-way from the door; Then He a-rose, o-ver
skies with His glo-ry will shine; Won-der-ful day, my be-

born of a vir-gin— Dwelt a-mong men, my ex-am-ple is He!
spised and re-ject-ed; Bear-ing our sins, my Re-deem-er is He!
tomb to keep vig-il; Hope of the hope-less, my Sav-iour is He!
death He had con-quered; Now is as-cend-ed, my Lord ev-er-more!
lov-ed ones bring-ing; Glo-ri-ous Sav-iour, this Je-sus is mine!

CHORUS

Liv-ing, He loved me; dy-ing, He saved me; Bur-ied, He

car-ried my sins far a-way; Ris-ing, He jus-ti-fied

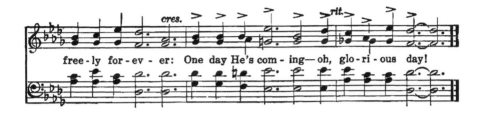

free - ly for - ev - er: One day He's com - ing—oh, glo - ri - ous day!

There is a fountain filled with blood 71

WILLIAM COWPER WILLIAM GARDINER

1. There is a foun - tain fill'd with blood Drawn from Im -
2. The dy - ing thief re - joiced to see That foun - tain
3. Dear dy - ing Lamb, Thy pre - cious blood Shall nev - er
4. E'er since, by faith, I saw the stream Thy flow - ing

man - uel's veins; And sin - ners, plunged be - neath that
in his day; And there may I, though vile as
lose its pow'r, Till all the ran - somed Church of
wounds sup - ply, Re - deem - ing love has been my

flood, Lose all their guilt - y stains.
he, Wash all my sins a - way,
God Be saved, to sin no more,
theme, And shall be till I die, A - men.

HORATIUS BONAR   JOHN B. DYKES

1. I heard the voice of Je - sus say, "Come un - to Me and rest;
2. I heard the voice of Je - sus say, "Be - hold, I free - ly give
3. I heard the voice of Je - sus say, "I am this dark world's Light;

Org.

Lay down, thou wea - ry one, lay down Thy head up - on My breast."
The liv - ing wa - ter; thirst - y one, Stoop down, and drink, and live."
Look un - to Me, thy morn shall rise, And all thy day be bright."

I came to Je - sus as I was, Wea - ry and worn and sad;
I came to Je - sus and I drank Of that life - giv - ing stream;
I looked to Je - sus, and I found In Him my Star, my Sun;

I found in Him a rest - ing place, And He has made me glad.
My thirst was quenched, my soul revived, And now I live in Him.
And in that light of life I'll walk, Till travel - ing days are done. A-men.

E. J. BELLERBY   TUNE OF HYMN 72

1. Shine on me, O Lord Jesus,
  And let me ever know
The grace that shone from Calvary,
  Where Thou didst love me so.
"My child, I am thy Saviour.
  'Tis not what thou dost feel,
But Mine own gracious promise,
  Which does thy pardon seal."

2. Shine in me, O Lord Jesus,
  And let Thy searching light
Reveal each hidden purpose,
  . Each thought as in Thy sight.
"My child, I am thy Searcher,
  I try each loving heart,
For I would have most holy
  All who in Me have part."

3. Shine through me then, Lord Jesus,
  That all the world may see
The life I live is Thy life,
  'And thus be drawn to Thee.

"My child, I am thy Power;
  With those who hear My voice
I ever dwell, and use them,
  Thus making them rejoice."

4. Shine out, shine out, Lord Jesus,
  Thou Light of all the world;
Oh, let Thy Gospel banner
  Be everywhere unfurled!
"My child, hast thou forgotten
  That name is also thine?
My fruit is borne on branches,
  Not by the parent Vine."

5. Arise and shine, Lord Jesus,
  Thou Bright and Morning Star;
I long for Thine appearing,
  When peace shall follow war.
"My child, before I gather
  My family in one,
Its number needs completing;
  T'wards this, what hast thou
    done?"

Jesus, Thy blood and righteousness

7

NICOLAUS L. ZINZENDORF (JOHN WESLEY, TR.)   LUDWIG VON BEETHOVEN

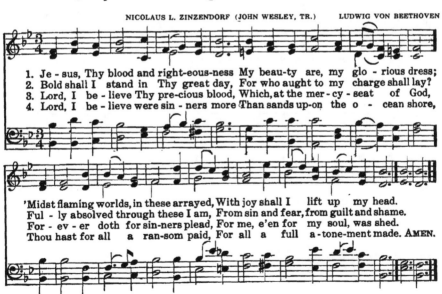

1. Je - sus, Thy blood and right-eous-ness My beau-ty are, my glo - rious dress;
2. Bold shall I stand in Thy great day, For who aught to my charge shall lay?
3. Lord, I be - lieve Thy pre-cious blood, Which, at the mer - cy - seat of God,
4. Lord, I be - lieve were sin - ners more Than sands up-on the o - cean shore,

'Midst flaming worlds, in these arrayed, With joy shall I lift up my head.
Ful - ly absolved through these I am, From sin and fear, from guilt and shame.
For - ev - er doth for sin-ners plead, For me, e'en for my soul, was shed.
Thou hast for all a ran-som paid, For all a full a - tone-ment made. AMEN.

PRISCILLA J. OWENS   WILLIAM J. KIRKPATRICK

1. We have heard a joy-ful sound, Je - sus saves, Je - sus saves;
2. Waft it on the roll - ing tide, Je - sus saves, Je - sus saves;
3. Sing a - bove the bat - tle's strife, Je - sus saves, Je - sus saves;
4. Give the winds a might - y voice Je - sus saves, Je - sus saves;

Spread the glad - ness all a - round, Je - sus saves, Je - sus saves;
Tell to sin - ners, far and wide, Je - sus saves, Je - sus saves;
By His death and end - less life, Je - sus saves, Je - sus saves;
Let the na - tions now re - joice, Je - sus saves, Je - sus saves;

Bear the news to ev - ry land, Climb the steeps, and cross the waves,
Sing, ye is - lands of the sea, Ech - o back, ye o - cean caves,
Sing it soft - ly thro' the gloom, When the heart for mer - cy craves,
Shout sal - va - tion, full and free, High - est hills and deep - est caves,

On - ward, 'tis our Lord's com-mand, Je - sus saves, Je - sus saves.
Earth shall keep her ju - bi - lee, Je - sus saves, Je - sus saves.
Sing in tri - umph o'er the tomb, Je - sus saves, Je - sus saves.
This our song of vic - to - ry, Je - sus saves, Je - sus saves. A - MEN.

JOHN M. WIGNER   FREDERICK C. MAKER

1. Come to the Sav - iour now! He gen - tly call - eth thee;
2. Come to the Sav - iour now! Gaze on that cleans - ing tide—
3. Come to the Sav - iour now! He suf - fered all for thee;
4. Come to the Sav - iour, all! What - e'er your bur - dens be;

In true re - pent - ance bow, Be - fore Him bend the knee:
Wa - ter and blood that flow Forth from His wound - ed side.
And in His mer - its thou Hast an un - fail - ing plea:
Hear now His lov - ing call "Cast all your care on Me."

He wait - eth to be - stow Sal - va - tion, peace, and love,
Hark to the suf - f'ring One: "'Tis fin - ished!" now He cries:
No vain ex - cus - es frame, For feel - ings do not stay;
Come, and for ev - 'ry grief In Je - sus you will find

True joy on earth be - low, A home in heav'n a - bove.
Re - demp - tion's work is done, Then bows His head and dies.
None who to Je - sus came Were ev - er sent a - way.
A sure and safe re - lief, A lov - ing Friend and kind. A - men.

Jesus may come today

GEORGE W. WHITCOMB   CHARLES H. MARSH

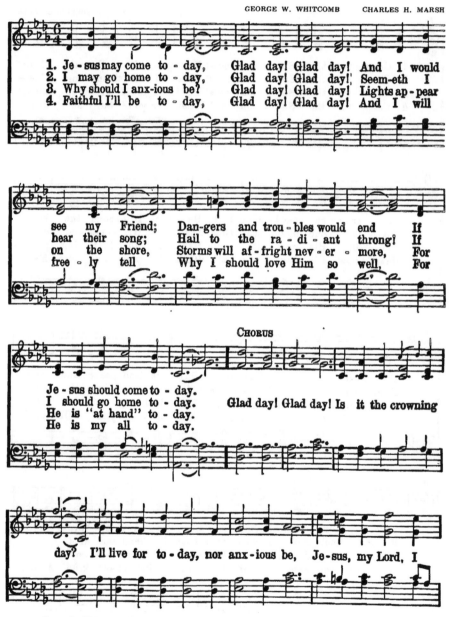

1. Je - sus may come to - day, Glad day! Glad day! And I would
2. I may go home to - day, Glad day! Glad day! Seem-eth I
3. Why should I anx-ious be? Glad day! Glad day! Lights ap - pear
4. Faithful I'll be to - day, Glad day! Glad day! And I will

see my Friend; Dan-gers and trou - bles would end If
hear their song; Hail to the ra - di - ant throng? If
on the shore, Storms will af - fright nev - er - more, For
free - ly tell Why I should love Him so well, For

CHORUS

Je - sus should come to - day.
I should go home to - day.
He is "at hand" to - day.   Glad day! Glad day! Is it the crowning
He is my all to - day.

day? I'll live for to - day, nor anx-ious be, Je-sus, my Lord, I

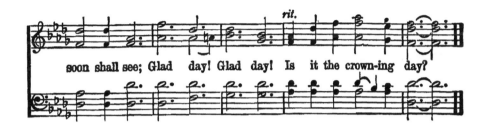

soon shall see; Glad day! Glad day! Is it the crown-ing day?

Rock of ages, cleft for me

AUGUSTUS M. TOPLADY   THOMAS HASTINGS

1. Rock of A - ges, cleft for me, Let me hide my - self in Thee;
2. Not the la - bors of my hands Can ful - fill Thy law's de - mands;
3. Noth - ing in my hand I bring, Sim - ply to Thy cross I cling;
4. While I draw this fleet - ing breath, When mine eyes shall close in death,

Let the wa - ter and the blood, From Thy riv - en side which flowed,
Could my zeal no res - pite know, Could my tears for - ev - er flow,
Na - ked, come to Thee for dress, Help - less, look to Thee for grace;
When I soar to worlds un - known, See Thee on Thy judg-ment-throne.

Be of sin the dou - ble cure, Cleanse me from its guilt and power.
All for sin could not a - tone; Thou must save, and Thou a - lone.
Foul, I to the foun - tain fly, Wash me, Sav - iour, or I die!
Rock of A - ges, cleft for me, Let me hide my - self in Thee. A-MEN.

Hail to the brightness of Zion's glad morning

THOMAS HASTINGS   LOWELL MASON

1. Hail to the bright-ness of Zi - on's glad morn - ing,
2. Hail to the bright-ness of Zi - on's glad morn - ing,
3. Lo, in the des - ert rich flow - ers are spring - ing,
4. See, from all lands, from the isles of the o - cean,

Joy to the lands that in dark - ness have lain!
Long by the proph - ets of Is - rael fore - told;
Streams ev - er co - pious are flow - ing a - long;
Praise to the Sav - iour as - cend - ing on high;

Hushed be the ac - cents of sor - row and mourn - ing,
Hail to the mil - lions from bond - age re - turn - ing!
Loud from the moun - tain - tops ech - oes are ring - ing,
Fall - en the wea - pons of war and com - mo - tion,

Zi - on in tri - umph be - gins her mild reign.
Gen - tiles and Jews the blest vi - sion be - hold.
Wastes rise in ver - dure and min - gle in song.
Shouts of sal - va - tion are rend - ing the sky. A - MEN.

MARY A. THOMSON   JAMES WALCH

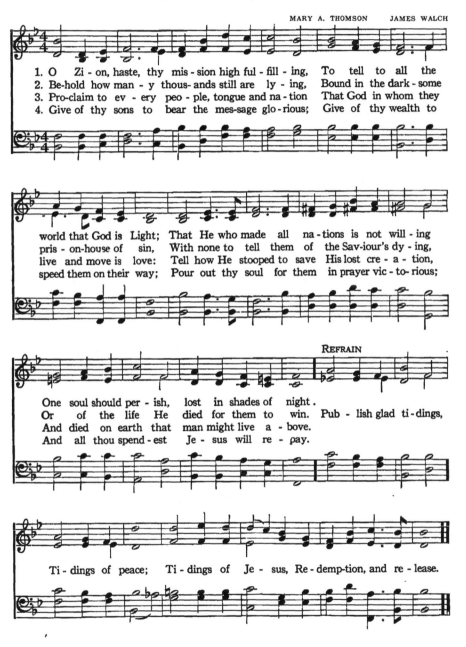

1. O Zi-on, haste, thy mis-sion high ful-fill-ing, To tell to all the
2. Be-hold how man-y thous-ands still are ly-ing, Bound in the dark-some
3. Pro-claim to ev-ery peo-ple, tongue and na-tion That God in whom they
4. Give of thy sons to bear the mes-sage glo-rious; Give of thy wealth to

world that God is Light; That He who made all na-tions is not will-ing
pris-on-house of sin, With none to tell them of the Sav-iour's dy-ing,
live and move is love: Tell how He stooped to save His lost cre-a-tion,
speed them on their way; Pour out thy soul for them in prayer vic-to-rious;

REFRAIN

One soul should per-ish, lost in shades of night.
Or of the life He died for them to win. Pub-lish glad ti-dings,
And died on earth that man might live a-bove.
And all thou spend-est Je-sus will re-pay.

Ti-dings of peace; Ti-dings of Je-sus, Re-demp-tion, and re-lease.

ELISHA A. HOFFMAN   ELISHA A. HOFFMAN

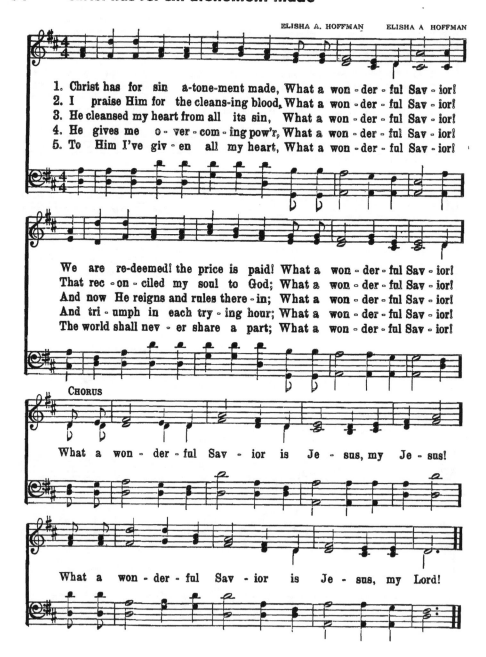

1. Christ has for sin a-tone-ment made, What a won-der-ful Sav-ior!
2. I praise Him for the cleans-ing blood, What a won-der-ful Sav-ior!
3. He cleansed my heart from all its sin, What a won-der-ful Sav-ior!
4. He gives me o-ver-com-ing pow'r, What a won-der-ful Sav-ior!
5. To Him I've giv-en all my heart, What a won-der-ful Sav-ior!

We are re-deemed! the price is paid! What a won-der-ful Sav-ior!
That rec-on-ciled my soul to God; What a won-der-ful Sav-ior!
And now He reigns and rules there-in; What a won-der-ful Sav-ior!
And tri-umph in each try-ing hour; What a won-der-ful Sav-ior!
The world shall nev-er share a part; What a won-der-ful Sav-ior!

CHORUS

What a won-der-ful Sav-ior is Je-sus, my Je-sus!

What a won-der-ful Sav-ior is Je-sus, my Lord!

E H. BICKERSTETH   TUNE OF HYMN 19

1. "For My sake and the Gospel's, go
   And tell Redemption's story";
   His heralds answer, "Be it so,
   And Thine, Lord, all the glory!"
   They preach His birth, His life,
       His cross,
   The love of His atonement,
   For whom they count the world
       but loss,
   His Easter, His enthronement.

2. Hark, hark! the trump of Jubilee
   Proclaims to ev'ry nation,
   From pole to pole, by land and sea,
   Glad tidings of salvation:
   As nearer draws the day of doom,
   While still the battle rages,
   The heavenly Dayspring thro'
       the gloom
   Breaks on the night of ages.

3. Still on and on the anthems spread
   Of hallelujah voices,
   In concert with the holy dead
   The warrior church rejoices:
   Their snow-white robes are washed
       in blood,
   Their golden harps are ringing;
   Earth and the Paradise of God
   One triumph song are singing.

4. He comes, whose advent trumpet
       drowns
   The last of Time's evangels.
   Emmanuel crowned with many
       crowns,
   The Lord of saints and angels:
   O Life, Light, Love, the great I AM,
   Triune, who changest never,
   The throne of God and of the Lamb
   Is Thine, and Thine for ever!

Art thou weary, art thou languid?   83

GREEK HYMN (JOHN M. NEALE. TR.)   HENRY W. BAKER

1. Art thou wea - ry, art thou lan - guid, Art thou sore dis-tressed?
2. Hath He marks to lead me to Him, If He be my guide?
3. Is there di - a - dem, as mon - arch, That His brow a - dorns?
4. If I find Him, if I fol - low, What His guer - don here?
5. If I still hold close - ly to Him, What hath He at last?

'Come to me, saith One, 'and com - ing, Be at rest.'
In His feet and hands are wound-prints, And His side.
Yea, a crown in ver - y sure - ty, But of thorns.
Many a sor - row, many a la - bor, Many a tear.
Sor - row van-quished, la - bor end - ed, Jor - dan passed.   A-MEN.

6 If I ask Him to receive me,
   Will He say me nay?
   Not till earth, and not till heaven
   Pass away.

7 Finding, following, keeping, struggling,
   Is He sure to bless?
   Saints, apostles, prophets, martyrs,
   Answer, 'Yes.'

84   *Eternal Light! Eternal Light!*

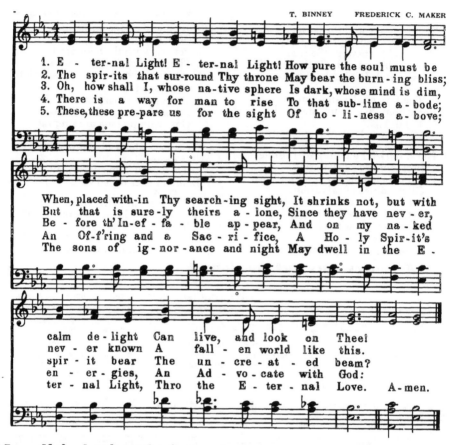

T. BINNEY   FREDERICK C. MAKER

1. E - ter-nal Light! E - ter-nal Light! How pure the soul must be
2. The spir-its that sur-round Thy throne May bear the burn-ing bliss;
3. Oh, how shall I, whose na-tive sphere Is dark, whose mind is dim,
4. There is a way for man to rise To that sub-lime a-bode;
5. These, these pre-pare us for the sight Of ho-li-ness a-bove;

When, placed with-in Thy search-ing sight, It shrinks not, but with
But that is sure-ly theirs a - lone, Since they have nev - er,
Be - fore th'In-ef - fa - ble ap-pear, And on my na-ked
An Of-f'ring and a Sac - ri - fice, A Ho - ly Spir-it's
The sons of ig - nor-ance and night May dwell in the E -

calm de - light Can live, and look on Thee!
nev - er known A fall - en world like this.
spir - it bear The un - cre - at - ed beam?
en - er - gies, An Ad - vo - cate with God:
ter - nal Light, Thro the E - ter - nal Love. A-men.

85   *If the Lord my Saviour comes*

MARIETTA C. PRINCE.   LEWIS S. CHAFER

1. If the Lord my Sav - iour comes, At the dawn - ing,
2. If the Lord my Sav - iour comes, At the noon time
3. If the Lord my Sav - iour comes, In the shad - ows
4. If the Lord my Sav - iour comes, In the qui - et

By permission of Lewis S. Chafer

In the morn-ing, Of a gold-en sum-mer day, Will He
In the hur-ry, 'Mid the toil and press-ing care, Will I
Of the twi-light, When the cares are laid a-side, Will He
Of the mid-night, When the earth is hushed to rest, Will He

find me wait-ing, watch-ing, For His call to come a-way?
hear His sweet voice call-ing, Hear that shout-ing in the air?
find my soul still hark-ing, For His sum-mons to His bride?
find my lamp all read-y, Bid me en-ter with the blest?

I hear the words of love

HORATIUS BONAR FROM THE GENEVAN PSALTER

1. I hear the words of love, I gaze up-on the blood, I
2. 'Tis ev-er last-ing peace! Sure as Je-ho-vah's Name; 'Tis
3. The clouds may come and go, And storms may sweep my sky This
4. My love is oft-times low, My joy still ebbs and flows; But
5. I change, He chang-es not, The Christ can nev-er die; His

see the might-y sac-ri-fice And I have peace with God.
sta-ble as His stead-fast throne, For ev-er-more the same.
blood-seal'd friend-ship chang-es not: The cross is ev-er nigh.
peace with Him re-mains the same No change Je-ho-vah knows.
love, not mine, the rest-ing place, His truth, not mine, the tie. A-men.

WADE ROBINSON   J. MOUNTAIN

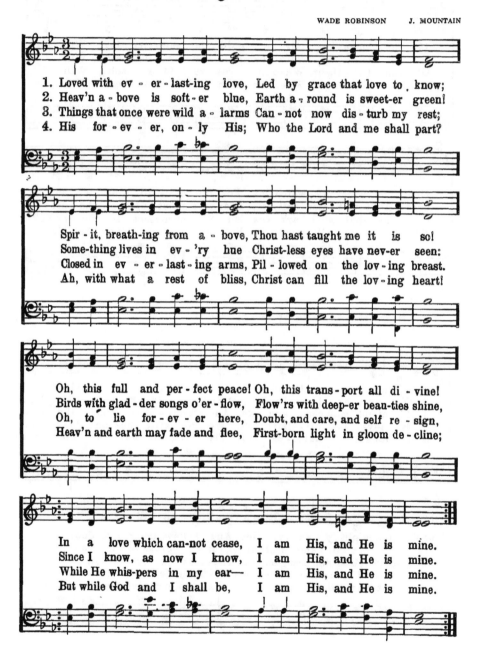

1. Loved with ev - er - last-ing love, Led by grace that love to know;
2. Heav'n a - bove is soft - er blue, Earth a - round is sweet-er green!
3. Things that once were wild a - larms Can - not now dis - turb my rest;
4. His for - ev - er, on - ly His; Who the Lord and me shall part?

Spir - it, breath-ing from a - bove, Thou hast taught me it is so!
Some-thing lives in ev - 'ry hue Christ-less eyes have nev-er seen:
Closed in ev - er - last - ing arms, Pil - lowed on the lov-ing breast.
Ah, with what a rest of bliss, Christ can fill the lov-ing heart!

Oh, this full and per - fect peace! Oh, this trans - port all di - vine!
Birds with glad - der songs o'er - flow, Flow'rs with deep-er beau-ties shine,
Oh, to lie for - ev - er here, Doubt, and care, and self re - sign,
Heav'n and earth may fade and flee, First-born light in gloom de - cline;

In a love which can-not cease, I am His, and He is mine.
Since I know, as now I know, I am His, and He is mine.
While He whis-pers in my ear— I am His, and He is mine.
But while God and I shall be, I am His, and He is mine.

When you pray

WHEN YOU pray individually or in prayer groups, you will want to use these hymns. In singing a hymn of prayer, you make it possible for the entire group to enter into the same prayer. In this section are included hymns for preparation for prayer as well as those which set forth the doctrine of prayer as it is in the Scriptures.

Every prayer meeting should contain an element of praise . . . a prayer meeting may be altogether a praise service, a time when you do not *ask* God for anything. For such an emphasis, see also two other sections, "When you gather for Christian fellowship," which begins with song 1, and "When you want to know God better," which begins with song 107.

Breathe on me, breath of God

EDWIN HATCH · ROBERT JACKSON

1. Breathe on me, Breath of God, Fill me with life a-new, That I may
2. Breathe on me, Breath of God, Un-til my heart is pure, Un-til with
3. Breathe on me, Breath of God, Till I am whol-ly Thine, Till all this
4. Breathe on me, Breath of God, So shall I nev-er die, But live with

love what Thou dost love, And do what Thou wouldst do.
Thee I will one will, To do or to en-dure.
earth-ly part of me Glows with Thy fire di-vine.
Thee the per-fect life Of Thine e-ter-ni-ty. A-MEN.

Music by permission of Mrs. Ethel Taylor

89   Come, ye disconsolate

THOMAS MOORE   SAMUEL WEBBE

1. Come, ye dis - con - so - late, wher - e'er ye lan - guish, Come to the
2. Joy of the des - o - late, Light of the stray - ing, Hope of the
3. Here see the Bread of Life; see wa - ters flow - ing Forth from the

mer - cy seat, fer - vent - ly kneel! Here bring your wound - ed hearts,
pen - i - tent, fade - less and pure! Here speaks the Com - fort - er,
throne of God, pure from a - bove: Come to the feast of love;

here tell your an - guish: Earth has no sor - row that heaven can - not heal.
ten - der - ly say - ing, "Earth has no sor - row that heaven can - not cure.
come, ev - er know - ing Earth has no sor - row but heaven can re - move. A. MEN.

90   Our blest Redeemer, ere He breathed

HARRIET AUBER   JOHN B DYKES

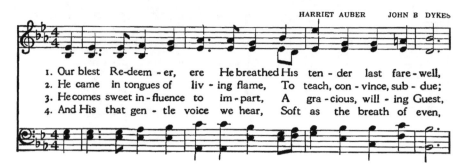

1. Our blest Re-deem - er, ere He breathed His ten - der last fare - well,
2. He came in tongues of liv - ing flame, To teach, con - vince, sub - due;
3. He comes sweet in - fluence to im - part, A gra - cious, will - ing Guest,
4. And His that gen - tle voice we hear, Soft as the breath of even,

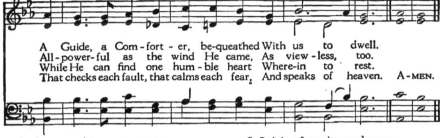

A Guide, a Com-fort-er, be-queathed With us to dwell.
All-power-ful as the wind He came, As view-less, too.
While He can find one hum-ble heart Where-in to rest.
That checks each fault, that calms each fear, And speaks of heaven. A-MEN.

5. And every virtue we possess,
   And every victory won,
   And every thought of holiness
   Are His alone.

6. Spirit of purity and grace,
   Our weakness, pitying see:
   O make our hearts Thy dwelling place,
   And worthier Thee!

Come, my soul, thy suit prepare

91

JOHN NEWTON   XAVIER SCHNYDER

1. Come, my soul, thy suit pre-pare: Je-sus loves to an-swer prayer;
2. Thou art com-ing to a King, Large pe-ti-tions with thee bring;
3. With my bur-den I be-gin: Lord, re-move this load of sin;
4. Lord, I come to Thee for rest, Take pos-ses-sion of my breast;

He Him-self has bid thee pray, There-fore will not say thee nay.
For His grace and power are such, None can ev-er ask too much.
Let Thy blood, for sin-ners spilt, Set my con-science free from guilt.
There Thy blood-bought right main-tain, And with-out a ri-val reign. A-men.

5. While I am a pilgrim here,
   Let Thy love my spirit cheer;
   As my Guide, my Guard, my Friend,
   Lead me to my journey's end.

6. Show me what I have to do,
   Every hour my strength renew:
   Let me live a life of faith,
   Let me die Thy people's death.

JOSEPH SCRIVEN   CHARLES C. CONVERSE

1. What a friend we have in Je - sus, All our sins and griefs to bear;
2. Have we tri - als and temp-ta - tions? Is there trou-ble an - y-where?
3. Are we weak and heav - y - la - den, Cum-bered with a load of care?

What a priv - i - lege to car - ry Ev - ery-thing to God in prayer'
We should nev - er be dis - cour - aged; Take it to the Lord in prayer.
Pre - cious Sav - iour, still our ref - uge; Take it to the Lord in prayer.

O what peace we oft - en for - feit, O what need-less pain we bear,
Can we find a friend so faith - ful. Who will all our sor-rows share?
Do thy friends des-pise, for - sake thee? Take it to the Lord in prayer;

All be-cause we do not car - ry Ev - ery-thing to God in prayer.
Je - sus knows our ev - ery weak-ness; Take it to the Lord in prayer.
In His arms He'll take and shield thee, Thou wilt find a sol-ace there. A-MEN.

Arise, my soul, arise

CHARLES WESLEY   TRADITIONAL AMERICAN MELODY

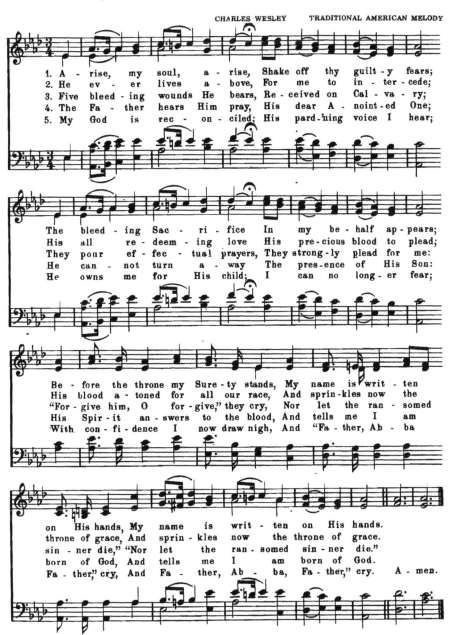

1. A - rise, my soul, a - rise, Shake off thy guilt - y fears;
2. He ev - er lives a - bove, For me to in - ter - cede;
3. Five bleed - ing wounds He bears, Re - ceived on Cal - va - ry;
4. The Fa - ther hears Him pray, His dear A - noint - ed One;
5. My God is rec - on - ciled; His pard - 'ning voice I hear;

The bleed - ing Sac - ri - fice In my be - half ap - pears;
His all re - deem - ing love His pre - cious blood to plead;
They pour ef - fec - tual prayers, They strong - ly plead for me:
He can - not turn a - way The pres - ence of His Son:
He owns me for His child; I can no long - er fear;

Be - fore the throne my Sure - ty stands, My name is writ - ten
His blood a - toned for all our race, And sprin - kles now the
"For - give him, O for - give," they cry, Nor let the ran - somed
His Spir - it an - swers to the blood, And tells me I am
With con - fi - dence I now draw nigh, And "Fa - ther, Ab - ba

on His hands, My name is writ - ten on His hands.
throne of grace, And sprin - kles now the throne of grace.
sin - ner die," "Nor let the ran - somed sin - ner die."
born of God, And tells me I am born of God.
Fa - ther," cry, And Fa - ther, Ab - ba, Fa - ther," cry. A - men.

94 Approach, my soul, the mercy-seat

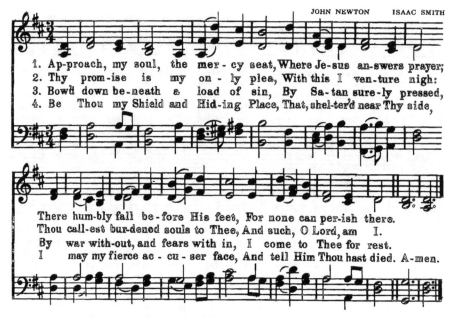

JOHN NEWTON   ISAAC SMITH

1. Ap-proach, my soul, the mer-cy seat, Where Je-sus an-swers prayer;
2. Thy prom-ise is my on-ly plea, With this I ven-ture nigh:
3. Bow'd down be-neath a load of sin, By Sa-tan sure-ly pressed,
4. Be Thou my Shield and Hid-ing Place, That, shel-ter'd near Thy side,

There hum-bly fall be-fore His feet, For none can per-ish there.
Thou call-est bur-dened souls to Thee, And such, O Lord, am I.
By war with-out, and fears with in, I come to Thee for rest.
I may my fierce ac-cu-ser face, And tell Him Thou hast died. A-men.

5. O wondrous love, to bleed and die,
To bear the Cross and shame,
That guilty sinners, such as I,
Might plead Thy gracious Name!

95 Prayer is the soul's sincere desire

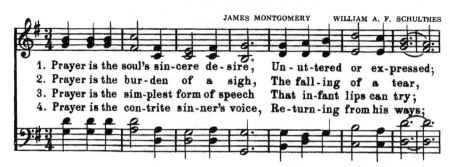

JAMES MONTGOMERY   WILLIAM A. F. SCHULTHES

1. Prayer is the soul's sin-cere de-sire, Un-ut-tered or ex-pressed;
2. Prayer is the bur-den of a sigh, The fall-ing of a tear,
3. Prayer is the sim-plest form of speech That in-fant lips can try;
4. Prayer is the con-trite sin-ner's voice, Re-turn-ing from his ways;

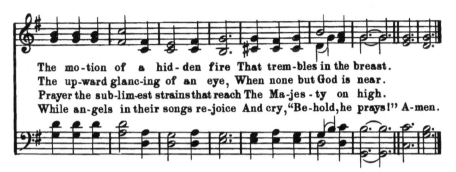

The mo-tion of a hid-den fire That trem-bles in the breast.
The up-ward glanc-ing of an eye, When none but God is near.
Prayer the sub-lim-est strains that reach The Ma-jes-ty on high.
While an-gels in their songs re-joice And cry, "Be-hold, he prays!" A-men.

5. Prayer is the Christian's vital breath,
   The Christian's native air,
   His watchword at the gates of death;
   He enters heaven with prayer.

6. O Thou, by whom we come to God,
   The Life, the Truth, the Way;
   The path of prayer Thyself hast trod:
   Lord, teach us how to pray!

Speak, Lord, in the stillness

96

E MAY GRIMES   H GREEN

1. Speak, Lord, in the still - ness, While I wait on Thee;
2. Speak, O bless - ed Mas - ter, In this qui - et hour,
3. For the words Thou speak - est, "They are life" in - deed;
4. All to Thee is yield - ed, I am not my own;

Hushed my heart to lis - ten In ex - pec - tan - cy.
Let me see Thy face, Lord, Feel Thy touch of power.
Liv - ing Bread from heav - en, Now my spir - it feed!
Bliss - ful, glad sur - ren - der I am Thine a - lone. A - men.

5. Speak, Thy servant heareth!
   Be not silent, Lord:
   Waits my soul upon Thee
   For the quickening word!

6. Fill me with the knowledge
   Of Thy glorious will;
   All Thine own good pleasure
   In Thy child fulfil.

AVIS B. CHRISTIANSEN   HOMER HAMMONTREE

1. Fill all my vi-sion, Sav-iour, I pray, Let me see on-ly Je-sus to-day;
2. Fill all my vi-sion, ev-'ry de-sire Keep for Thy glo-ry; My soul in-spire
3. Fill all my vi-sion, let naught of sin Shad-ow the brightness shin-ing with-in.

Tho' thro' the val-ley Thou leadest me, Thy fade-less glo-ry en-com-pass-eth me.
With Thy per-fec-tion, Thy ho-ly love Flood-ing my pathway with light from a-bove.
Let me see on-ly Thy blessed face, Feast-ing my soul on Thy in-fi-nite grace.

CHORUS

Fill all my vi-sion, Sav-iour di-vine, Till with Thy glo-ry my spir-it shall shine.

Fill all my vi-sion, that all may see Thy Ho-ly Im-age re-flect-ed in me.

Copyright 1940 by Homer Hammontree

RAY PALMER   LOWELL MASON

1. My faith looks up to Thee, Thou Lamb of
2. May Thy rich grace im - part Strength to my
3. While life's dark maze I tread, And griefs a -
4. When ends life's tran - sient dream, When death's cold,

Cal - va - ry, Sav - iour di - vine: Now hear me
faint - ing heart, My zeal in - spire; As Thou hast
round me spread, Be Thou my Guide; Bid dark - ness
sul - len stream Shall o'er me roll, Blest Sav - iour,

while I pray, Take all my guilt a - way,
died for me, O may my love to Thee
turn to day, Wipe sor - row's tears a - way,
then, in love, Fear and dis - trust re - move;

O let me from this day Be whol - ly Thine!
Pure, warm, and change - less be, A liv - ing fire!
Nor let me ev - er stray From Thee a - side.
O bear me safe a - bove, A ran - somed soul! A-MEN.

Come, thou fount of every blessing

ROBERT ROBINSON   JOHN WYETH

1. Come, Thou Fount of ev - ery bless - ing, Tune my heart to sing Thy grace;
2. Here I raise mine Eb - en - e - zer; Hith - er by Thy help I'm come;
3. O to grace how great a debt - or Dai - ly I'm con-strained to be!

Streams of mer - cy, nev - er ceas - ing, Call for songs of loud - est praise.
And I hope, by Thy good pleas - ure, Safe - ly to ar - rive at home.
Let Thy good - ness, like a fet - ter, Bind my wan - dering heart to Thee:

Teach me some me - lo - dious son - net Sung by flam - ing tongues a - bove;
Je - sus sought me when a stran-ger, Wan - d'ring from the fold of God;
Prone to wan - der, Lord, I feel it, Prone to leave the God I love;

Praise the mount! I'm fixed up - on it, Mount of Thy re - deem-ing love.
He, to res - cue me from dan - ger, In - ter-posed His pre-cious blood.
Here's my heart, O take and seal it, Seal it for Thy courts a - bove. A - MEN.

When you search the Scriptures

W<small>HEN YOU</small> meet together to study the Bible, you will probably not want to do much singing, but rather confine yourself to the business at hand. You may not want to use more than one of the hymns from this section on the Word of God at any Bible study. The songs from the section "When you gather for Christian fellowship," can also be used.

A hymn about the Word of God can be used in any meeting which centers on the Scriptures. For instance, at a conference such a hymn could precede a message on Bible study, and any of them could very appropriately be used before the reading of the Scriptures in a worship service.

Lord, Thy Word abideth   100

H. W BAKER   FROM GESANGBUCH (W. H. MONK, ARR.)

1. Lord, Thy Word a - bid - eth, And our foot - steps guid - eth;
2. When our foes are near us, Then Thy Word doth cheer us,
3. When the storms are o'er us, And dark clouds be - fore us,
4. Who can tell the pleas - ure, Who re - count the treas - ure

Who its truth be - liev - eth Light and joy re - ceiv - eth.
Word of con - so - la - tion, Mes - sage of sal - va - tion.
Then its light di - rect - eth, And our way pro - tect - eth.
By the Word im - part - ed To the sim - ple heart - ed? A - men.

"K" IN JOHN RIPON'S SELECTION   TRADITIONAL AMERICAN MELODY

1. How firm a foun - da - tion, ye saints of the Lord,
2. "Fear not, I am with thee, O be not dis - mayed,
3. "When through the deep wa - ters I call thee to go,
4. "When through fier - y tri - als thy path - way shall lie,
5. "The soul that on Je - sus hath leaned for re - pose,

Is laid for your faith in His ex - cel - lent word!
For I am thy God, and will still give thee aid;
The riv - ers of sor - row shall not o - ver - flow;
My grace, all - suf - fi - cient, shall be thy sup - ply;
I will not, I will not de - sert to his foes;

What more can He say than to you He hath said,
I'll strength - en thee, help thee, and cause thee to stand,
For I will be with thee, thy trou - bles to bless,
The flame shall not hurt thee; I on - ly de - sign
That soul, though all hell should en - deav - or to shake,

To you who for ref - uge to Je - sus have fled.
Up - held by My right - eous, om - nip - o - tent hand.
And sanc - ti - fy to thee thy deep - est dis - tress.
Thy dross to con - sume, and thy gold to re - fine.
I'll nev - er, no nev - er, no nev - er for - sake!" A - MEN.

103   *Break Thou the Bread of life*

MARY A. LATHBURY   WILLIAM F. SHERWIN

1. Break Thou the bread of life, Dear Lord, to me, As Thou didst
2. Bless Thou the truth, dear Lord, To me— to me, As Thou didst
3. Thou art the bread of life, O Lord, to me, Thy ho - ly
4. O send Thy Spir - it, Lord, Now un - to me, That He may

break the loaves Be - side the sea; Be - yond the sa - cred page
bless the bread By Gal - i - lee; Then shall all bond - age cease,
Word the truth That sav - eth me; Give me to eat and live
touch my eyes, And make me see: Show me the truth con-cealed

I seek Thee, Lord, My spir - it pants for Thee, O liv - ing Word.
All fet - ters fall; And I shall find my peace, My All in all.
With Thee a - bove; Teach me to love Thy truth, For Thou art love.
With-in Thy Word, And in Thy Book re-vealed I see the Lord. A-MEN.

104   *Lamp of our feet, whereby we trace*

BERNARD D. BARTON   WILLIAM A. F. SCHULTHES

1. Lamp of our feet, where-by we trace Our path, when wont to stray;
2. Bread of our souls, where-on we feed, True man - na from on high;
3. Pil - lar of fire, through watch-es dark, Or ra-diant cloud by day;
4. Word of the ev - er liv - ing God, Will of His glo - rious Son;

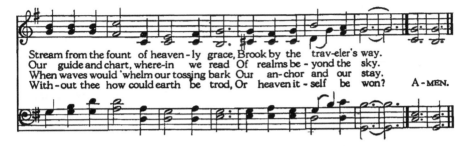

Stream from the fount of heaven-ly grace, Brook by the trav-eler's way.
Our guide and chart, where-in we read Of realms be-yond the sky.
When waves would 'whelm our tossing bark Our an-chor and our stay.
With-out thee how could earth be trod, Or heaven it-self be won? A-MEN.

God, in the gospel of His Son

BENJAMIN BEDDOME AND THOMAS COTTERILL   EDWARD MILLER

1. God, in the gos-pel of His Son, Makes His e-
2. Here sin-ners of a hum-ble frame May taste His
3. The pris-'ner here may break his chains; The wea-ry
4. O grant us grace, Al-might-y Lord, To read and

ter-nal coun-sels known; Where love in all its
grace and learn His name; May read in char-ac-
rest from all His pains; The cap-tive feel His
mark thy ho-ly word; Its truth with meek-ness

glo-ry shines, And truth is drawn in fair-est lines.
ters of blood, The wis-dom, pow'r and grace of God.
bond-age cease; The mourn-er find the way of peace.
to re-ceive, And by its ho-ly pre-cepts live.

Guide me, O Thou great Jehovah

WILLIAM WILLIAMS   JOHN HUGHES

1. Guide me, O Thou great Je - ho - vah, Pil - grim through this
2. O - pen now the crys - tal foun - tain, Whence the heal - ing
3. When I tread the verge of Jor - dan, Bid my anx - ious

bar - ren land; I am weak, but Thou art might-y; Hold me with Thy
stream doth flow; Let the fire and cloud-y pil - lar Lead me all my
fears sub-side; Death of death, and hell's de-struc-tion, Land me safe on

power - ful hand; Bread of heav - en, Bread of heav - en,
jour - ney through; Strong De - liv - er - er, strong De - liv - er - er,
Ca - naan's side; Songs of prais - es, songs of prais - es

Feed me till I want no more, Feed me till I want no more.
Be Thou still my strength and shield, Be Thou still my strength and shield.
I will ev - er give to Thee, I will ev - er give to Thee. A-MEN.

Music by permission of Mrs John Hughes

When you want to know God better

*T*HE DEEPEST hunger and yearning of the human soul redeemed by Christ is for an intimate, personal, experimental knowledge of God in Christ. When you want to express that longing, you will find a hymn in this section that will be appropriate. Through singing these hymns, you will gain a deeper longing for the heights which they express, and you will find that your desire is fulfilled in Christ.

These hymns are intensely personal. Use them in your "quiet time." They are not a substitute for the Scriptures, but you will find that many of them perfectly express your desire for fellowship with God. Memorize the words and make them your own. Use them also in prayer meetings, devotional meetings, and in your conferences, when the theme is a personal, intimate relationship with Christ. Many are also appropriate to sing when you meet together to observe the Lord's Supper.

Jesus, Thou Joy of loving hearts

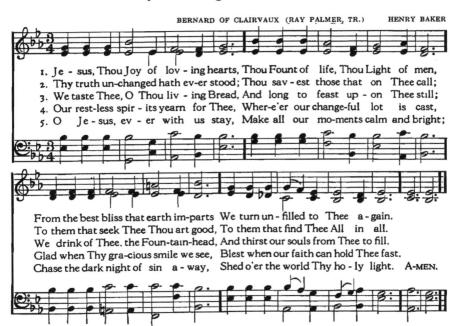

BERNARD OF CLAIRVAUX (RAY PALMER, TR.)　　　HENRY BAKER

1. Je - sus, Thou Joy of lov - ing hearts, Thou Fount of life, Thou Light of men,
2. Thy truth un–changed hath ev - er stood; Thou sav - est those that on Thee call;
3. We taste Thee, O Thou liv - ing Bread, And long to feast up - on Thee still;
4. Our rest-less spir - its yearn for Thee, Wher-e'er our change-ful lot is cast,
5. O Je - sus, ev - er with us stay, Make all our mo-ments calm and bright;

From the best bliss that earth im-parts We turn un - filled to Thee a - gain.
To them that seek Thee Thou art good, To them that find Thee All in all.
We drink of Thee, the Foun-tain-head, And thirst our souls from Thee to fill.
Glad when Thy gra-cious smile we see, Blest when our faith can hold Thee fast.
Chase the dark night of sin a - way, Shed o'er the world Thy ho - ly light. A-MEN.

Come, my soul, thou must be waking

F. R. L VON CANITZ (H. J. BUCKOLL, TR)   FRANZ JOSEPH HAYDN

1. Come, my soul, thou must be wak - ing; Now is
2. Glad - ly hail the sun re - turn - ing; Read - y
3. Pray that He may pros - per ev - er Each en -
4. Our God's boun - teous gifts a - buse not, Light re -

break - ing O'er the earth an - oth - er day:
burn - ing Be the in - cense of thy powers;
deav - or, When thine aim is good and true;
fuse not, But His Spir - it's voice o - bey;

Come to Him who made this splen - dor; See thou
For the night is safe - ly end - ed; God hath
But that He may ev - er thwart thee, And con -
Thou with Him shalt dwell, be - hold - ing Light en -

ren - der All thy fee - ble strength can pay.
tend - ed With His care thy help - less hours.
vert thee, When thou e - vil wouldst pur - sue.
fold - ing All things in un - cloud - ed day. A - MEN

CHARLES WESLEY   JOSEPH PARRY

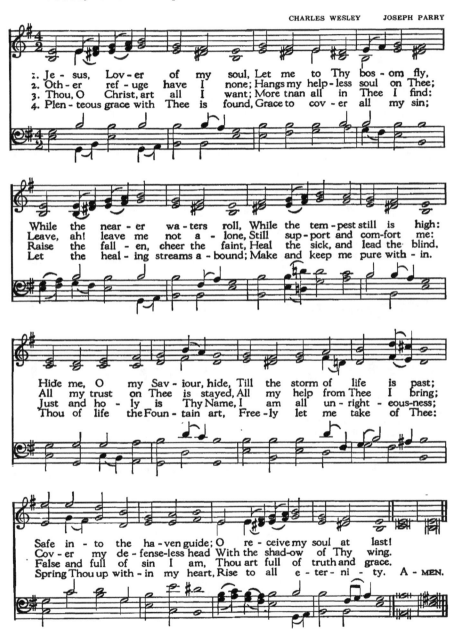

1. Je - sus, Lov - er of my soul, Let me to Thy bos - om fly,
2. Oth - er ref - uge have I none; Hangs my help - less soul on Thee;
3. Thou, O Christ, art all I want; More than all in Thee I find:
4. Plen - teous grace with Thee is found, Grace to cov - er all my sin;

While the near - er wa - ters roll, While the tem - pest still is high:
Leave, ah! leave me not a - lone, Still sup - port and com - fort me:
Raise the fall - en, cheer the faint, Heal the sick, and lead the blind.
Let the heal - ing streams a - bound; Make and keep me pure with - in.

Hide me, O my Sav - iour, hide, Till the storm of life is past;
All my trust on Thee is stayed, All my help from Thee I bring;
Just and ho - ly is Thy Name, I am all un - right - eous-ness;
Thou of life the Foun - tain art, Free - ly let me take of Thee:

Safe in - to the ha - ven guide; O re - ceive my soul at last!
Cov - er my de - fense-less head With the shad - ow of Thy wing.
False and full of sin I am, Thou art full of truth and grace.
Spring Thou up with - in my heart, Rise to all e - ter - ni - ty. A - MEN.

Music by permission of Hughes and Son, Publisher

Our day of praise is done

JOHN ELLERTON   JOSEPH JOWETT

1. Our day of praise is done, The eve - ning
2. A - round the throne . on high, Where night can
3. Too faint our an - thems here; Too soon of
4. Yet, Lord, to Thy dear will If Thou at -

shad - ows fall; But pass not from us with the
nev - er be, The white - robed har - pers of the
praise we tire: But O, the strains, how full and
tune the heart, We in Thine an - gels' mus - ic

sun, True Light that light - 'nest all.
sky Bring cease - less hymns to Thee.
clear, Of that e - ter - nal choir!
still May bear our low - er part. A - men.

5. 'Tis Thine each soul to calm,
   Each wayward thought reclaim,
   And make our life a daily psalm
   Of glory to Thy Name.

6. A little while, and then
   Shall come the glorious end;
   And songs of angels and of men
   In perfect praise shall blend.

When I survey the wondrous cross

ISAAC WATTS   LOWELL MASON

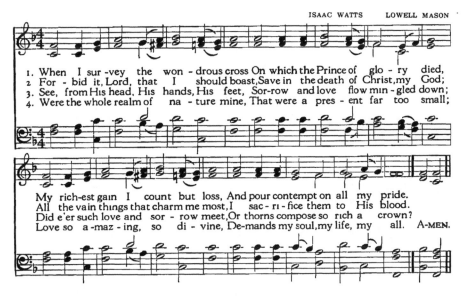

1. When I sur-vey the won-drous cross On which the Prince of glo-ry died,
2. For-bid it, Lord, that I should boast, Save in the death of Christ, my God;
3. See, from His head, His hands, His feet, Sor-row and love flow min-gled down;
4. Were the whole realm of na-ture mine, That were a pres-ent far too small;

My rich-est gain I count but loss, And pour contempt on all my pride.
All the vain things that charm me most, I sac-ri-fice them to His blood.
Did e'er such love and sor-row meet, Or thorns compose so rich a crown?
Love so a-maz-ing, so di-vine, De-mands my soul, my life, my all. A-MEN.

Saviour, breathe an evening blessing

JAMES EDMESTON   GEORGE C. STEBBINS

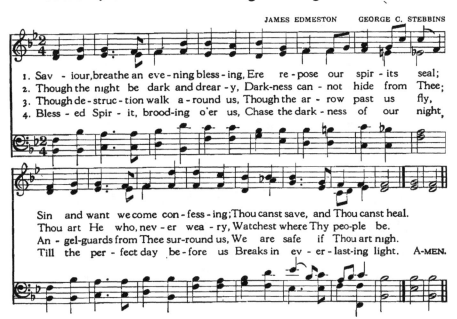

1. Sav-iour, breathe an eve-ning bless-ing, Ere re-pose our spir-its seal;
2. Though the night be dark and drear-y, Dark-ness can-not hide from Thee;
3. Though de-struc-tion walk a-round us, Though the ar-row past us fly,
4. Bless-ed Spir-it, brood-ing o'er us, Chase the dark-ness of our night,

Sin and want we come con-fess-ing; Thou canst save, and Thou canst heal.
Thou art He who, nev-er wea-ry, Watchest where Thy peo-ple be.
An-gel-guards from Thee sur-round us, We are safe if Thou art nigh.
Till the per-fect day be-fore us Breaks in ev-er-last-ing light. A-MEN.

Rise my soul, and stretch thy wings

ROBERT SEAGRAVE   JAMES NARES

1. Rise, my soul, and stretch thy wings, Thy bet-ter por-tion trace;
2. Ri-vers to the o-cean run, Nor stay in all their course;
3. Fly me rich-es, fly me cares, Whilst I that coast ex-plore;
4. Cease, ye pil-grims, cease to mourn, Press on-ward to the prize;

Rise from tran-si-to-ry things Towards heaven, thy na-tive place.
Fire as-cend-ing seeks the sun; Both speed them to their source:
Flat-tering world, with all thy snares, So-lic-it me no more.
Soon our Sav-iour will re-turn Tri-umph-ant in the skies:

Sun and moon and stars de-cay, Time shall soon this earth re-move;
So my soul, de-rived from God, Pants to view His glor-ious face,
Pil-grims fix not here their home; Stran-gers tar-ry but a night;
Yet a sea-son, and you know Hap-py en-trance will be given,

Rise, my soul, and haste a-way To seats pre-pared a-bove.
For-ward tends to His a-bode, To rest in His em-brace.
When the last dear morn is come, They'll rise to joy-ful light.
All our sor-rows left be-low, And earth ex-changed for heaven.

ANNIE R. COUSIN   IRA D. SANKEY

1. O Christ what bur-dens bow'd Thy head: Our load was laid on Thee; Thou
2. Death and the curse were in our cup: O Christ 'twas full for Thee! But
3. Je - ho - vah lift-ed up His rod: O Christ it fell on Thee! Thou
4. The tem-pest's aw-ful voice was heard; O Christ it broke on Thee! Thy

stood-est in the sin-ner's stead Did'st bear all ill for me. A
Thou hast drain'd the last dark drop, 'Tis emp-ty now for me: That
wast sore strick-en of Thy God; There's not one stroke for me. Thy
o - pen bo-som was my ward, It braved the storm for me. Thy

vic - tim led, Thy blood was shed! Now there's no load for me.
bit - ter cup, love drank it up, Now bles-sing's draught for me.
tears, Thy blood, be-neath it flowed; Thy bruising healeth me.
form was scarred Thy vi-sage marr'd, Now cloudless peace for me. A - men.

5. Jehovah bade His sword awake:
   O Christ, it woke 'gainst Thee;
Thy blood the flaming blade must slake,
   Thy heart its sheath must be.
All for my sake, my peace to make:
   Now sleeps that sword for me.

6. For me, Lord Jesus, Thou hast died,
   And I have died in Thee:
Thou'rt risen—my bands are all untied;
   And now Thou liv'st in me;
When purified, made white, and tried,
   Thy glory then for me.

115   *The day Thou gavest, Lord, is ended*

JOHN ELLERTON   CLEMENT C. SCHOLEFIELD

1. The day Thou gav - est, Lord, is end - ed, The dark - ness
2. We thank Thee that Thy Church un - sleep - ing, While earth rolls
3. As o'er each con - ti - nent and is - land The dawn leads
4. So be it, Lord; Thy throne shall nev - er, Like earth's proud

falls at Thy be - hest; To Thee our morn - ing hymns as -
on - ward in - to light, Through all the world her watch is
on an - oth - er day, The voice of prayer is nev - er
em - pires, pass a - way; Thy king - dom stands, and grows for

cend - ed, Thy praise shall hal - low now our rest.
keep - ing, And rests not now by day or night.
si - lent, Nor die the strains of praise a - way.
ev - er, Till all Thy crea - tures own Thy sway. A - MEN.

Music by permission of Oxford University Press

16   *I am not worthy, holy Lord*

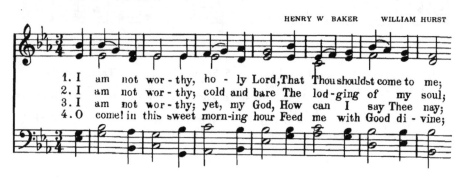

HENRY W BAKER   WILLIAM HURST

1. I am not wor - thy, ho - ly Lord, That Thou shouldst come to me;
2. I am not wor - thy; cold and bare The lod - ging of my soul;
3. I am not wor - thy; yet, my God, How can I say Thee nay;
4. O come! in this sweet morn - ing hour Feed me with Good di - vine;

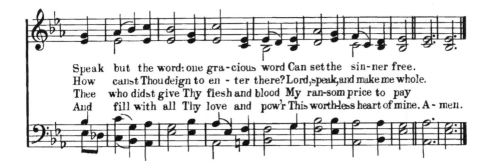

Speak but the word: one gra-cious word Can set the sin-ner free.
How canst Thou deign to en - ter there? Lord, speak, and make me whole.
Thee who didst give Thy flesh and blood My ran-som price to pay
And fill with all Thy love and pow'r This worth-less heart of mine. A - men.

Awake, my soul, and with the sun 117

THOMAS KEN   FRANCOIS H. BARTHELEMON

1. A - wake, my soul, and with the sun Thy dai - ly stage of du - ty run;
2. In con - ver - sa - tion be sin-cere, Keep con-science as the noon-day clear;
3. Wake, and lift up thy-self, my heart And with the an - gels bear thy part,
4. May I, like them, in God de-light; Have all day long my God in sight!

Shake off dull sloth, and joy-ful rise To pay thy morn-ing sa-cri-fice.
Think how all-see-ing God thy ways And all thy se-cret thots sur-veys.
Who all night long un-wearied sing High praise to the e - ter-nal King.
Per - form, like them, my Maker's will, And cel-e-brate His glo-ries still. A-men

5. Glory to Thee who safe hast kept,
And hast refreshed me whilst I slept;
Grant, Lord, when I from death shall wake,
I may of endless light partake.

6 Lord, I my vows to Thee renew;
Disperse my sins as morning dew;

Guard my first springs of thought and will,
And with Thyself my spirit fill.

7. Direct, control, suggest, this day,
All I design, or do, or say;
That all my powers, with all their might,
In Thy sole glory may unite.

FRANCES R. HAVERGAL   ETHELBERT W. BULLINGER

1. I am trust-ing Thee, Lord Je-sus, Trust-ing on-ly Thee;
2. I am trust-ing Thee to guide me, Thou a-lone shalt lead,
3. I am trust-ing Thee for pow-er: Thine can nev-er fail;
4. I am trust-ing Thee, Lord Je-sus; Nev-er let me fall;

Trust-ing Thee for full sal-va-tion, Great and free.
Ev-ery day and hour sup-ply-ing All my need.
Words which Thou Thy-self shalt give me Must pre-vail.
I am trust-ing Thee for-ev-er, And for all. A-MEN.

---

119   *Rise, my soul! behold, 'tis Jesus*

J. DENHAM SMITH   TUNE OF HYMN 67

1. Rise, my soul! behold, 'tis Jesus,
    Jesus fills thy wondering eyes;
 See Him now in glory seated,
    Where thy sins no more can rise.

2. There, in righteousness transcendent,
    Lo! He doth in heaven appear,
 Shows the blood of His atonement
    As thy title to be there.

3. All thy sins were laid upon Him,
    Jesus bore them on the tree;
 God, who knew them, laid them on Him,
    And, believing, thou art free.

4. God now brings thee to His dwelling,
    Spreads for thee His feast Divine,
 Bids thee welcome, ever telling
    What a portion there is thine.

5. In that circle of God's favor,
    Circle of the Father's love,
 All is rest, and rest for ever;
    All is perfectness above.

6. Blessed, glorious word "for ever!"
    Yea, "for ever!" is the word;
 Nothing can the ransomed sever;—
    Nought divide them from the Lord.

O sacred Head, once wounded

ANON. (P. GERHARDT AND J. ALEXANDER, TRS.)   H L. HASSLER (J S. BACH ARR.)

1. O sa - cred Head, once wound - ed, With grief and shame bow'd down,
2. What Thou, my Lord, hast suf - fered, Was all for sin - ners' gain;
3. What lan - guage shall I bor - row To thank Thee, dear - est Friend,
4. Be near me when I'm dy - ing, O show Thy cross to me;

Now scorn - ful - ly sur - round - ed With thorns, Thine on - ly crown.
Mine, mine was the trans - gres - sion, But Thine the dead - ly pain:
For this Thy dy - ing sor - row, Thy pi - ty with - out end?
And to my suc - cour fly - ing Come, Lord, and set me free.

O sa - cred Head, what glo - ry, What bliss till now was Thine!
Lo, here I fall, my Sav - iour! 'T is I de - serve Thy place;
O make me Thine for ev - er; And should I faint - ing be,
These eyes, new faith re - ceiv - ing, From Je - sus shall not move;

Yet, though de - spised and go - ry, I joy to call Thee mine.
Look on me with Thy fa - vor, Vouch-safe to me Thy grace.
Lord, let me nev - er, nev - er Out - live my love for Thee.
For he, who dies be - liev - ing, Dies safe - ly through Thy love.

Jesus, I am resting, resting

JEAN S. PIGOTT   J. MOUNTAIN

1. Je - sus! I am rest - ing, rest - ing In the joy of what Thou art;
2. Oh, how great Thy lov - ing kind-ness, Vas - ter, broader than the sea!
3. Sim - ply trust - ing Thee, Lord Je - sus, I be - hold Thee as Thou art,
4. Ev - er lift Thy face up - on me, As I work and wait for Thee;

Refrain: Je - sus, I am rest - ing, rest - ing, In the joy of what Thou art;

Fine

I am find - ing out the great-ness Of Thy lov - ing heart.
Oh, how mar - vel - lous Thy good-ness, Lav-ished all on me!
And Thy love so pure, so change-less, Sat - is - fies my heart;
Rest - ing 'neath Thy smile, Lord Je - sus, Earth's dark shad-ows flee.
I am find - ing out the great-ness Of Thy lov - ing heart.

Thou hast bid me gaze up - on Thee, And Thy beau - ty fills my soul,
Yes, I rest in Thee, Be - lov - ed, Know what wealth of grace is Thine,
Sat - is - fies its deep-est long-ings, Meets, supplies its ev - 'ry need,
Bright-ness of my Fa-ther's glo - ry, Sun - shine of my Fa-ther's face,

D.C.

For, by Thy trans - form - ing pow - er, Thou hast made me whole.
Know Thy cer - tain - ty of prom - ise, And have made it mine.
Com - pass-eth me 'round with bless - ings: Thine is love in - deed!
Keep me ev - er trust - ing, rest - ing, Fill me with Thy grace.

JOHN S B MONSELL   ANON.

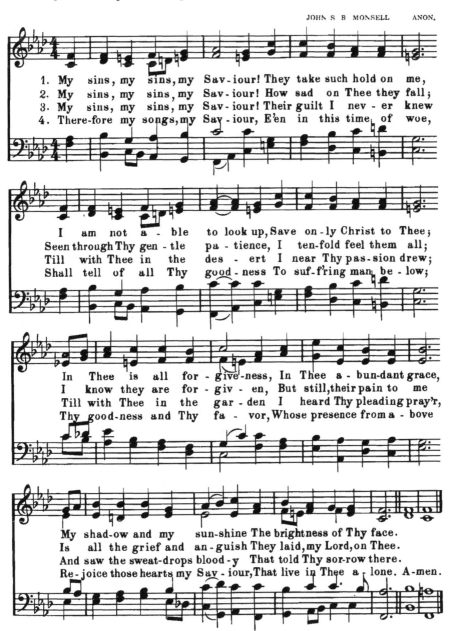

1. My sins, my sins, my Sav-iour! They take such hold on me,
2. My sins, my sins, my Sav-iour! How sad on Thee they fall;
3. My sins, my sins, my Sav-iour! Their guilt I nev-er knew
4. There-fore my songs, my Sav-iour, E'en in this time of woe,

I am not a - ble to look up, Save on-ly Christ to Thee;
Seen through Thy gen - tle pa - tience, I ten-fold feel them all;
Till with Thee in the des - ert I near Thy pas-sion drew;
Shall tell of all Thy good - ness To suf-f'ring man be - low;

In Thee is all for - give-ness, In Thee a - bun-dant grace,
I know they are for - giv - en, But still, their pain to me
Till with Thee in the gar - den I heard Thy pleading pray'r,
Thy good-ness and Thy fa - vor, Whose presence from a - bove

My shad-ow and my sun-shine The brightness of Thy face.
Is all the grief and an - guish They laid, my Lord, on Thee.
And saw the sweat-drops blood-y That told Thy sor-row there.
Re - joice those hearts my Sav - iour, That live in Thee a - lone. A-men.

123   *Fairest Lord Jesus*

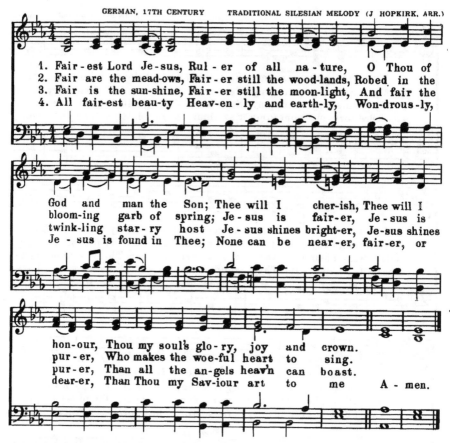

GERMAN, 17TH CENTURY   TRADITIONAL SILESIAN MELODY (J HOPKIRK, ARR.)

1. Fair-est Lord Je-sus, Rul-er of all na-ture, O Thou of
2. Fair are the mead-ows, Fair-er still the wood-lands, Robed in the
3. Fair is the sun-shine, Fair-er still the moon-light, And fair the
4. All fair-est beau-ty Heav-en-ly and earth-ly, Won-drous-ly,

God and man the Son; Thee will I cher-ish, Thee will I
bloom-ing garb of spring; Je-sus is fair-er, Je-sus is
twink-ling star-ry host Je-sus shines bright-er, Je-sus shines
Je-sus is found in Thee; None can be near-er, fair-er, or

hon-our, Thou my soul's glo-ry, joy and crown.
pur-er, Who makes the woe-ful heart to sing.
pur-er, Than all the an-gels heav'n can boast.
dear-er, Than Thou my Sav-iour art to me A-men.

Music by permission of James Hopkirk

124   *May the grace of Christ our Saviour*

JOHN NEWTON   TUNE OF HYMN 112

1. May the grace of Christ our Saviour,
   And the Father's boundless love,
With the Holy Spirit's favor,
   Rest upon us from above.

2. Thus may we abide in union
   With each other and the Lord;
And possess, in sweet communion,
   Joys which earth cannot afford.

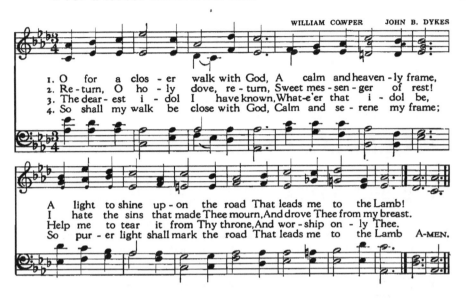

WILLIAM COWPER   JOHN B. DYKES

1. O for a clos - er walk with God, A calm and heaven - ly frame,
2. Re - turn, O ho - ly dove, re - turn, Sweet mes - sen - ger of rest!
3. The dear - est i - dol I have known, What-e'er that i - dol be,
4. So shall my walk be close with God, Calm and se - rene my frame;

A light to shine up - on the road That leads me to the Lamb!
I hate the sins that made Thee mourn, And drove Thee from my breast.
Help me to tear it from Thy throne, And wor - ship on - ly Thee.
So pur - er light shall mark the road That leads me to the Lamb A-MEN.

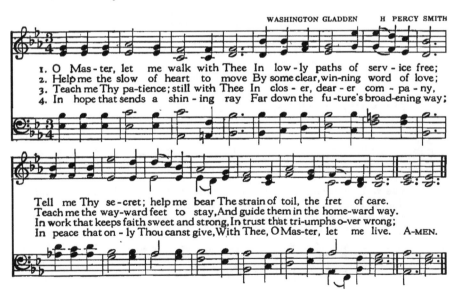

WASHINGTON GLADDEN   H PERCY SMITH

1. O Mas - ter, let me walk with Thee In low - ly paths of serv - ice free;
2. Help me the slow of heart to move By some clear, win - ning word of love;
3. Teach me Thy pa - tience; still with Thee In clos - er, dear - er com - pa - ny,
4. In hope that sends a shin - ing ray Far down the fu - ture's broad-ening way;

Tell me Thy se - cret; help me bear The strain of toil, the fret of care.
Teach me the way-ward feet to stay, And guide them in the home-ward way.
In work that keeps faith sweet and strong, In trust that tri-umphs o - ver wrong;
In peace that on - ly Thou canst give, With Thee, O Mas-ter, let me live. A-MEN.

O, my Saviour, crucified!

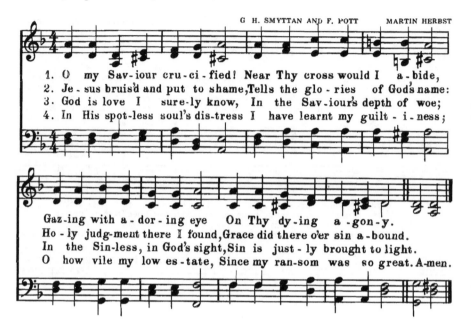

G. H. SMYTTAN AND F. POTT   MARTIN HERBST

1. O my Sav-iour cru-ci-fied! Near Thy cross would I a-bide,
2. Je-sus bruis'd and put to shame, Tells the glo-ries of God's name:
3. God is love I sure-ly know, In the Sav-iour's depth of woe;
4. In His spot-less soul's dis-tress I have learnt my guilt-i-ness;

Gaz-ing with a-dor-ing eye On Thy dy-ing a-gon-y.
Ho-ly judg-ment there I found, Grace did there o'er sin a-bound.
In the Sin-less, in God's sight, Sin is just-ly brought to light.
O how vile my low es-tate, Since my ran-som was so great. A-men.

5. Rent the veil that closed the way
   To my home of heav'nly day,
   In the flesh of Christ the Lord;
   Ever be His name adored!

6. Yet in sight of Calvary,
   Contrite should my spirit be,—
   Rest and holiness there find,
   Fashioned like my Saviour's mind.

The veil is rent! Lo, Jesus stands

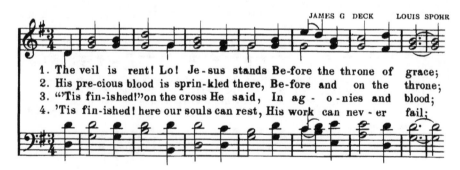

JAMES G DECK   LOUIS SPOHR

1. The veil is rent! Lo! Je-sus stands Be-fore the throne of grace;
2. His pre-cious blood is sprin-kled there, Be-fore and on the throne;
3. "'Tis fin-ished!" on the cross He said, In ag-o-nies and blood;
4. 'Tis fin-ished! here our souls can rest, His work can nev-er fail;

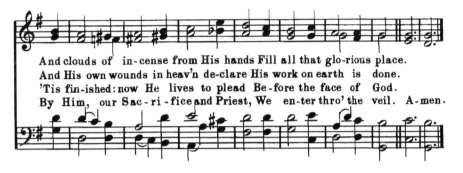

And clouds of in-cense from His hands Fill all that glo-rious place.
And His own wounds in heav'n de-clare His work on earth is done.
'Tis fin-ished: now He lives to plead Be-fore the face of God.
By Him, our Sac-ri-fice and Priest, We en-ter thro' the veil. A-men.

All for Jesus! 129

MARY D JAMES   JOHN STAINER

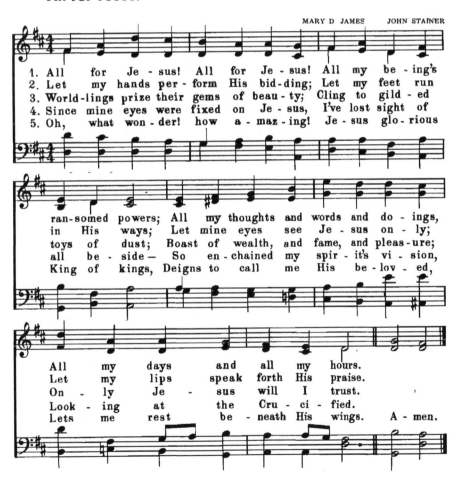

1. All for Je-sus! All for Je-sus! All my be-ing's
2. Let my hands per-form His bid-ding; Let my feet run
3. World-lings prize their gems of beau-ty; Cling to gild-ed
4. Since mine eyes were fixed on Je-sus, I've lost sight of
5. Oh, what won-der! how a-maz-ing! Je-sus glo-rious

ran-somed powers; All my thoughts and words and do-ings,
in His ways; Let mine eyes see Je-sus on-ly;
toys of dust; Boast of wealth, and fame, and pleas-ure;
all be-side— So en-chained my spir-it's vi-sion,
King of kings, Deigns to call me His be-lov-ed,

All my days and all my hours.
Let my lips speak forth His praise.
On-ly Je-sus will I trust.
Look-ing at the Cru-ci-fied.
Lets me rest be-neath His wings. A-men.

130   *May the mind of Christ my Saviour*

KATIE B. WILKINSON   A. CYRIL BARHAM GOULD

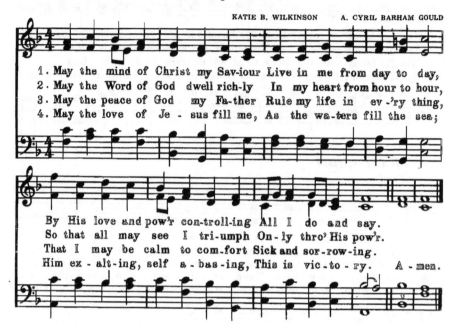

1. May the mind of Christ my Sav-iour Live in me from day to day,
2. May the Word of God dwell rich-ly In my heart from hour to hour,
3. May the peace of God my Fa-ther Rule my life in ev-'ry thing,
4. May the love of Je-sus fill me, As the wa-ters fill the sea;

By His love and pow'r con-troll-ing All I do and say.
So that all may see I tri-umph On-ly thro' His pow'r.
That I may be calm to com-fort Sick and sor-row-ing.
Him ex-alt-ing, self a-bas-ing, This is vic-to-ry. A-men.

5. May I run the race before me,
   Strong and brave to face the foe,
Looking only unto Jesus
   As I onward go.

6. May His beauty rest upon me
   As I seek the lost to win,
And may they forget the channel,
   Seeing only Him.

Words and music by permission of C. Barham Gould

131   *Teach me Thy way, O Lord*

B MANSELL RAMSEY   B. MANSELL RAMSEY

1. Teach me Thy Way, O Lord; Teach me Thy Way! Thy guid-ing grace af-ford;
2. When I am sad at heart, Teach me Thy Way! When earthly joys de-part,
3. When doubts and fears a-rise; Teach me Thy Way! When storms o'er spread the skies;
4. Long as my life shall last; Teach me Thy Way! Where'er my lot be cast;

By permission of John T. Park

Teach me Thy Way! Help me to walk a-right, more by faith
Teach me Thy Way! In hours of lone - li-ness, in times of
Teach me Thy Way! Shine through the cloud and rain, thro' sor - row,
Teach me Thy Way! Un - til the race is run, un - til the

less by sight, Lead me with heav'n-ly light; Teach me Thy way!
dire dis-tress, In fail_ure or suc-cess, Teach me Thy Way!
toil and pain, Make Thou my path-way plain; Teach me Thy Way!
jour-ney's done, Un - til the Crown is won; Teach me Thy Way! A - men.

Let me come closer to Thee, Jesus

132

J. L LYNE   J. H. LESTER

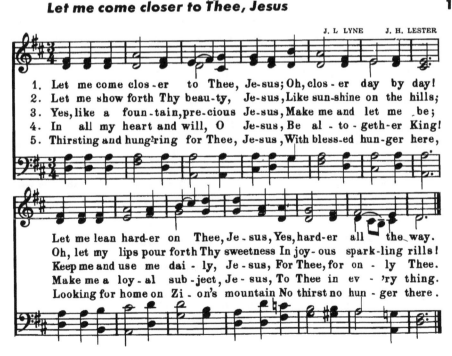

1. Let me come clos - er to Thee, Je-sus; Oh, clos - er day by day!
2. Let me show forth Thy beau-ty, Je-sus, Like sun-shine on the hills;
3. Yes, like a foun-tain, pre-cious Jesus, Make me and let me be;
4. In all my heart and will, O Jesus, Be al - to-geth-er King!
5. Thirsting and hung'ring for Thee, Je-sus, With bless-ed hun-ger here,

Let me lean hard-er on Thee, Je-sus, Yes, hard-er all the way.
Oh, let my lips pour forth Thy sweetness In joy-ous spark-ling rills!
Keep me and use me dai - ly, Je-sus, For Thee, for on - ly Thee.
Make me a loy-al sub-ject, Je-sus, To Thee in ev - 'ry thing.
Looking for home on Zi - on's mountain No thirst no hun - ger there.

Here, O my Lord, I see Thee face to face

HORATIUS BONAR   JAMES LANGRAN

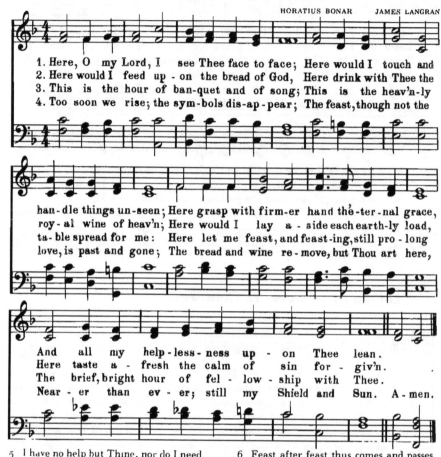

1. Here, O my Lord, I   see Thee face to face; Here would I touch and
2. Here would I feed up - on the bread of God, Here drink with Thee the
3. This is the hour of ban-quet and of song; This is the heav'n-ly
4. Too soon we rise; the sym-bols dis-ap-pear; The feast, though not the

han-dle things un-seen; Here grasp with firm-er hand the-ter-nal grace,
roy - al wine of heav'n; Here would I lay a - side each earth-ly load,
ta- ble spread for me: Here let me feast, and feast-ing, still pro - long
love, is past and gone; The bread and wine re-move, but Thou art here,

And   all   my help - less - ness up - on Thee lean.
Here taste a - fresh the calm of sin for - giv'n.
The brief, bright hour of fel - low - ship with Thee.
Near - er than ev - er; still my Shield and Sun. A - men.

5 I have no help but Thine, nor do I need
   Another arm save Thine to lean
   upon,
   It is enough, my Lord, enough indeed,
   My strength is in Thy might, Thy
   might alone

6 Feast after feast thus comes and passes
   by.
   Yet passing, points to the glad feast
   above,
   Giving sweet foretaste of the festal joy,
   The Lamb's great bridal feast of bliss
   and love.

Not what I am, O Lord, but what Thou art

HORATIUS BONAR   TUNE OF HYMN 133

1. Not what I am, O Lord, but what Thou art!
   That, that alone, can be my soul's true rest;
   Thy love, not mine, bids fear and doubt depart,
   And stills the tempest of my tossing breast.

2. It is Thy perfect love that casts out fear;
    I know the voice that speaks the "It is I,"
    And in these well-known words of heavenly cheer
    I hear the joy that bids each sorrow fly.

3. Thy Name is Love! I hear it from yon cross;
    Thy Name is Love! I read it in yon tomb;
    All meaner love is perishable dross,
    But this shall light me through time's thickest gloom.

4 It blesses now, and shall for ever bless;
    It saves me now, and shall for ever save;
    It holds me up in days of helplessness;
    It bears me safely o'er each swelling wave.

5. 'Tis what I know of Thee, my Lord and God,
    That fills my soul with peace, my lips with song;
    Thou art my health, my joy, my staff, my rod;
    Leaning on Thee, in weakness I am strong.

6. More of Thyself, oh, show me hour by hour;
    More of Thy glory, O my God and Lord;
    More of Thyself, in all Thy grace and power;
    More of Thy love and truth, Incarnate Word.

Take my life, and let it be　　　　　　　　　　13

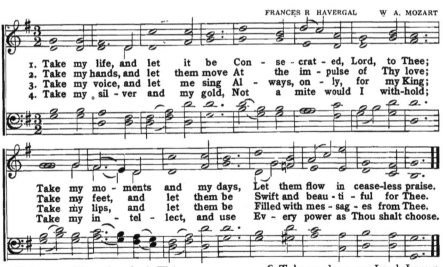

5. Take my will, and make it Thine,
    It shall be no longer mine;
    Take my heart, it is Thine own,
    It shall be Thy royal throne.

6. Take my love, my Lord, I pour
    At Thy feet its treasure store;
    Take myself, and I will be,
    Ever, only, all for Thee.

136 *Jesus, the very thought of Thee*

BERNARD OF CLAIRVAUX (EDWARD CASWALL, TR.)　JOHN B. DYKES

1. Je - sus, the ver - y thought of Thee With sweet-ness fills my breast;
2. Nor voice can sing, nor heart can frame, Nor can the mem - ory find
3. O Hope of ev - ery con - trite heart, O Joy of all the meek,
4. But what to those who find? Ah, this Nor tongue nor pen can show:
5. Je - sus, our on - ly Joy be Thou, As Thou our Prize wilt be;

But sweet-er far Thy face to see, And in Thy pres - ence rest.
A sweet-er sound than Thy blest Name, O Sav-iour of man-kind!
To those who fall, how kind Thou art! How good to those who seek!
The love of Je - sus, what it is None but His loved ones know.
Je - sus, be Thou our Glo - ry now, And through e - ter - ni - ty. A - MEN.

137 *Oh, teach me what it meaneth*

LUCY A. BENNETT　　TUNE OF HYMN 16

1. Oh, teach me what it meaneth—
That cross uplifted high,
With One—the Man of Sorrows—
Condemned to bleed and die!
Oh, teach me what it cost Thee
To make a sinner whole;
And teach me, Saviour, teach me
The value of a soul!

2. Oh, teach me what it meaneth—
That sacred crimson tide—
The blood and water flowing
From Thine own wounded side
Teach me that if none other
Had sinned, but I alone,
Yet still, Thy blood, Lord Jesus,
Thine only, must atone.

3. Oh, teach me what it meaneth—
Thy love beyond compare,
The love that reacheth deeper
Than depths of self-despair!

Yea, teach me, till there gloweth
In this cold heart of mine
Some feeble, pale reflection
Of that pure love of Thine.

4. Oh, teach me what it meaneth,
For I am full of sin;
And grace alone can reach me,
And love alone can win.
Oh, teach me, for I need Thee—
I have no hope beside,—
The chief of all the sinners
For whom the Saviour died!

5. O Infinite Redeemer!
I bring no other plea,
Because Thou dost invite me,
I cast myself on Thee.
Because Thou dost accept me,
I love and I adore;
Because Thy love constraineth,
I'll praise Thee evermore!

By permission of Marshall, Morgan and Scott, Ltd.

According to Thy gracious Word

JAMES MONTGOMERY   GREATOREX' "COLLECTION"

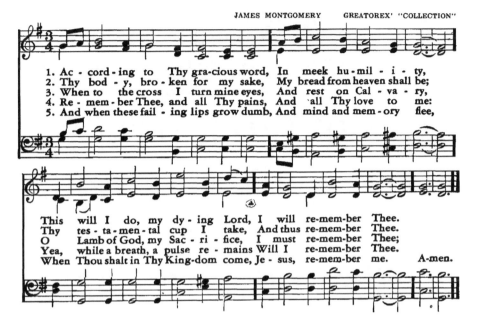

1. Ac - cord - ing to   Thy gra-cious word, In   meek hu - mil - i - ty,
2. Thy bod - y, bro - ken for my sake, My bread from heaven shall be;
3. When to   the cross I turn mine eyes, And rest on Cal - va - ry,
4. Re - mem - ber Thee, and all Thy pains, And all Thy love to   me:
5. And when these fail - ing lips grow dumb, And mind and mem - ory   flee,

This will I do, my dy - ing Lord, I   will re-mem-ber Thee.
Thy   tes - ta - men - tal cup I   take, And thus re-mem-ber Thee.
O   Lamb of God, my Sac - ri - fice, I must re-mem-ber Thee;
Yea, while a breath, a pulse re - mains Will I   re-mem-ber Thee.
When Thou shalt in Thy King-dom come, Je - sus, re-mem-ber me.   A-men.

Lord Jesus Christ, we seek Thy face

ALEXANDER STEWART   TUNE OF HYMN 15 OR 111

1. Lord Jesus Christ, we seek Thy face;
   Within the veil we bow the knee,
   Oh, let Thy glory fill the place,
   And bless us while we wait on Thee.

2. We thank Thee for the precious blood
   That purged our sins and brought us nigh,
   All cleansed and sanctified to God,
   Thy holy Name to magnify.

3. Shut in with Thee far, far above
   The restless world that wars below,
   We seek to learn and prove Thy love,
   Thy wisdom and Thy grace to know.

4. The brow that once with thorns was bound,
   Thy hands, Thy side, we fain would see,
   Draw near, Lord Jesus, glory-crowned,
   And bless us while we wait on Thee.

BERNARD OF CLAIRVAUX (EDWARD CASWALL, TR.)   ISAAC SMITH

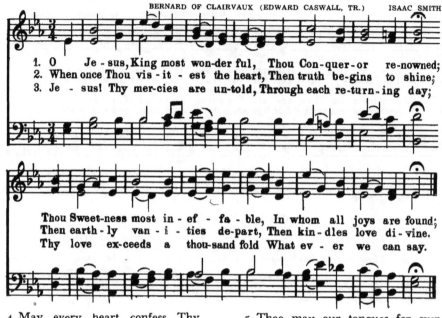

1. O   Je - sus, King most won-der-ful, Thou Con-quer-or   re-nowned;
2. When once Thou vis - it - est the heart, Then truth be-gins   to shine;
3. Je - sus! Thy mer-cies are un-told, Through each re-turn-ing day;

Thou Sweet-ness most in - ef - fa - ble, In whom all joys are found;
Then earth-ly van - i - ties de-part, Then kin-dles love di - vine.
Thy love ex-ceeds a   thou-sand fold What ev - er   we can say.

4. May every heart confess Thy
    Name,
    And ever Thee adore;
    And, seeking Thee, itself inflame
    And seek Thee more and more.

5. Thee may our tongues for ever
    bless;
    Thee may we love alone:
    And ever in our lives express
    The image of Thine own.

JOHANN SCHEFFLER (JOHN WESLEY, TR.)   HENRY CAREY

1. Thee will I   love, my strength, my tow'r, Thee will I   love, my
2. I   thank Thee un - cre - a - ted Sun That thy bright beams on
3. Up - hold me   in   the doubt-ful race, Nor suf - fer   me   a -
4. Thee will I   love, my joy, my crown; Thee will I   love, my

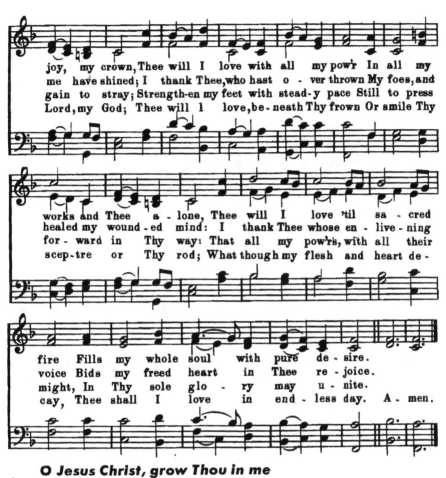

joy, my crown, Thee will I love with all my pow'r In all my
me have shined; I thank Thee, who hast o - ver thrown My foes, and
gain to stray; Strength-en my feet with stead-y pace Still to press
Lord, my God; Thee will I love, be-neath Thy frown Or smile Thy

works and Thee a - lone, Thee will I love 'til sa - cred
healed my wound - ed mind: I thank Thee whose en - live - ning
for - ward in Thy way: That all my pow'rs, with all their
scep-tre or Thy rod; What though my flesh and heart de -

fire Fills my whole soul with pure de - sire.
voice Bids my freed heart in Thee re - joice.
might, In Thy sole glo - ry may u - nite.
cay, Thee shall I love in end - less day. A - men.

O Jesus Christ, grow Thou in me 142

J. C. LAVATER (H. B. SMITH, TR)　　TUNE OF HYMN 138

1. O Jesus Christ, grow Thou in me,
   And all things else recede!
   My heart be daily nearer Thee,
   From sin be daily freed.

2. Each day let Thy supporting might
   My weakness still embrace;
   My darkness vanish in Thy light,
   Thy life my death efface.

3. In Thy bright beams which on me fall,
   Fade every evil thought;
   That I am nothing, Thou art all,
   I would be daily taught.

4. More of Thy glory let me see.
   Thou Holy, Wise, and True!
   I would Thy living image be,
   In joy and sorrow too.

5. Fill me with gladness from above,
   Hold me by strength Divine;
   Lord, let the glow of Thy great love
   Through my whole being shine.

6. Make this poor self grow less and less,
   Be Thou my life and aim;
   Oh, make me daily through Thy grace,
   More meet to bear Thy name!

143 *I am the Lord's! O joy beyond expression*

LUCY A. BENNETT   JOSEPH BARNBY

1. I am the Lord's! O joy be-yond ex-pres-sion, O sweet re-
sponse to voice of love Di-vine; Faith's joy-ous "Yes" to the as-sur-ing
whis-per, "Fear not! I have re-deem'd thee; thou art Mine."

2. I am the Lord's! It is the glad con-fes-sion, Where-with the
Bride re-calls the hap-py day, When love's "I will" ac-cept-ed Him for-
ev - er, "The Lord's," to love, to hon - or and o - bey.

3. I am the Lord's! Yet teach me all it mean-eth, All it in-
volves of love and loy-al - ty, Of ho - ly serv-ice, ab-so-lute sur-
ren - der, And un - re-served o - be-dience un - to Thee.

4. I am the Lord's! Yes; bod - y soul, and spir - it, O seal them
ir - re - cov - er - a-bly Thine; As Thou, Be-lov-ed, in Thy grace and
ful - ness For - ev - er and for - ev - er-more art mine. A-men.

Music by permission of Novello and Company, Ltd.

144 *Jesus, I live to Thee*

ROBERT JACKSON   TUNE OF HYMN 88

1. Jesus, I live to Thee,
   The Loveliest and Best;
   My life in Thee, Thy life in me,
   In Thy blest love I rest.

2. Jesus, I die to Thee,
   Whenever death shall come;
   To die in Thee is life to me
   In my eternal home.

3. Whether to live or die,
   I know not which is best;
   To live in Thee is bliss to me,
   To die is endless rest.

4. Living or dying, Lord,
   I ask but to be Thine;
   My life in Thee, Thy life in me,
   Makes heaven forever mine.

We come, O Christ to Thee

E. Margaret Clarkson   TUNE OF HYMN 34

1. We come, O Christ to Thee,
     True Son of God and man,
   By Whom all things consist,
     In Whom all life began:
        In Thee alone we live and move
        And have our being in Thy love.

2. Thou art the Way to God,
     Thy Blood our ransom paid;
   In Thee we face our Judge
     And Maker unafraid.
        Before the Throne absolved we stand:
        Thy love has met Thy Law's demand.

3. Thou art the living Truth!
     All wisdom dwells in Thee,
   Thou Source of every skill,
     Eternal Verity!
        Thou great I Am! In Thee we rest,
        True answer to our every quest.

4. Thou only art true Life,
     To know Thee is to live
   The more abundant life
     That earth can never give:
        O Risen Lord! We live in Thee
        And Thou in us eternally!

5. We worship Thee Lord Christ,
     Our Saviour and our King,
   To Thee our youth and strength
     Adoringly we bring:
        So fill our hearts that men may see
        Thy life in us and turn to Thee!

Index

W hen you are in a hurry, remember that hymns similar in subject are grouped together in this book. Where titles differ from first lines of the hymns, they have been indicated in the index by capitals.

CPSIA information can be obtained
at www.ICGtesting.com
Printed in the USA
BVHW03s1141010518
514943BV00012B/71/P

9 781258 448738